A Love That Never Fails

1 corinthians 13

guidelines
for LIVING

A Love That
Never Fails

| 1 corinthians 13 |

H. Dale Burke

MOODY PRESS
CHICAGO

All Scripture quotations, unless indicated, are taken from the *New American Standard Bible,* © 1960, 1962, 1963, 1968, 1971, 1972, 1973, 1975, 1977, and 1994 by The Lockman Foundation, La Habra, Calif. Used by permission.

Scripture quotations marked (NIV) are taken from the *Holy Bible: New International Version®.* NIV®. Copyright © 1973, 1978, 1984 by International Bible Society. Used by permission of Zondervan Publishing House. All rights reserved.

The "NIV" and "New International Version" trademarks are registered in the United States Patent and Trademark Office by International Bible Society. Use of either trademark requires permission of International Bible Society.

Scripture quotations marked (NEB) are taken from the *New English Bible* © 1961, 1970 by the Delegates of the Oxford University Press and the Syndics of the Cambridge University Press. All rights reserved.

Scripture quotations marked (KJV) are taken from the King James Version.

ISBN: 0-8024-8198-1

3 5 7 9 10 8 6 4 2

Printed in the United States of America

This year, 1999, I will celebrate twenty-five years
of marriage to the girl of my dreams.
To you, Becky Burke,
I dedicate this book on God's art of loving.
Without your love and the lessons
we have learned together,
this book would never have been written.
And to my three great gifts from God—
Beth, Paul, and Jaime—
I pray you see your dad in this book.
Thanks for the "love lessons" you've taught me.
Every father should be so blessed!

Contents

Foreword

Love is the longest entry in *Webster's New World Dictionary of Quotable Definitions*. For ten columns of small print writers from Byron to Balzac and Shakespeare to Shelly take a stab at defining the word *love*. Everything from the ridiculous ("Love is sentimental measles") to the sublime ("Love is a mutual self-giving which ends in self-recovery") takes a bow. But the big question goes unanswered: What is love?

When I was a freshman in college my speech teacher assigned each member of our class to give a short talk explaining or defining something commonly recognized. He added only one caveat to this simple assignment: "I don't want anyone to try to define what love is. I've heard enough freshman speeches trying to answer that question."

As a "student of the 60's," this was a challenge my latent rebelliousness could not resist. I thought, *I'll give a speech using First Corinthians Thirteen as my base and call it "What Love Is Not."* Somehow I recalled that of the fourteen defining statements the apostle Paul makes in his great chapter on love, most of them are negatives, i.e., what love is not. By rephrasing the others in a negative form ("love is not impatient . . . love is not unkind"), I was able to make my speech defining love by the use of negatives, thus meeting the teacher's assignment as well as circumventing his caveat.

Throughout the twentieth century there has certainly been no shortage of books about love, and all the great ones are each in their own way actually creative footnotes to the apostle's revelation of love that continues to speak from the thirteenth chapter of 1 Corinthians to each new generation. H. Dale Burke, following in this great tradition, offers his own new work on love for the twenty-first-century reader. Yet, it, too, is based on the eternal verities given in the first century to a group of new believers in the Greek city of Corinth.

In this fine book, Dale gives us a straightforward and practical treatise on love, developing the richness and insight of the apostle's inspired positive *and* negative truths about a subject that goes beyond even faith and hope in greatness.

As good as it is, Dale's book also is not the last word on love. But it is definitely a valuable one to reach for profitable enrichment and growth in the knowledge of the One who is Himself the First and Last word on the subject. The very same One who tells us, "Because I have loved you, you must love one another" with *a love that never fails.*

PAUL SAILHAMER
EXECUTIVE DIRECTOR
THE SERVANTS' TRUST
ANAHEIM, CALIFORNIA

Acknowledgments

For twenty years I have served as a senior pastor in God's church. It is my calling, my gift, and prayerfully, my contribution to the kingdom. I love it because at its heart it is the weekly study and delivery of truth. Exploring God's Word and delivering what I have discovered by God's grace is my passion and my privilege. In old-fashioned terms, I love to preach.

Upon coming to the Fullerton church, I met Jac La Tour. Jac shared my passion for the truth, but whereas I love to speak it, he loves to write it! In Jac I found a friend and a teammate for this project. Thank you, Jac, for encouraging and assisting me in my first effort to bring the spoken word to print. Without your gifts, this book would still be only a dream. It has truly been a joint venture that became an adventure worth repeating.

Your friend,
Dale

Introduction

Like most of their competitors, Ford Motor Company knows what people are looking for. Whether it's cars or coffeepots, consumers are tired of buying lemons. Ford's executives know that most of us have only so much money to spend, and we want to use those limited resources wisely. So what did Ford's marketing department tell us a few years ago? "Quality is Job One." Why? Because that slogan speaks straight to every car buyer's two most important questions. First, will it work? And second, will it last?

What's true for the cars we buy is true for the lives we live. People are looking for answers to life's questions. And there's no shortage of options on the market. Fads and philosophies abound, filling the bookshelves and airways with promises that seem to make sense . . . for the short term. But when tested over time, they don't hold up. In the midst of history's greatest wealth and largest libraries, with seemingly thousands of therapies and easy solutions, we find ourselves setting records we are not proud to hold. Divorce, depression, suicide, child and spousal abuse, crime, drug and alcohol abuse, and pornography are all on the rise, along with record debts on a dizzying array of credit cards. We spend more, travel more, enjoy more leisure time than any culture of times past, but life just doesn't seem to work. At least not very well.

Where can we go? Where can we look to find the key to successful living? We can do so much, know so much, access so much information so quickly, but we just can't seem to find the secret.

Maybe it's time we went back to school on the basics, time we sought and studied the skill that Jesus places at the center of all of life. I'm talking about the foundation on which every relationship rests. *Love.* After all, the apostle Paul says in 1 Corinthians 13 that "love never fails."

Jesus set the stage of Paul's letter to the Corinthians, and from Jesus' own mouth we hear the principles of His Father's brand of love—the love of which Paul writes.

Jesus tells us that *love is the great commandment,* summarizing God's entire law.

> *"You shall love the Lord your God with all your heart, and with all your soul, and with all your mind'... and...'You shall love your neighbor as yourself.'" (Matthew 22:37, 39)*

"Love God and love people" is the short version of how He put it. Then He said, "On these two commandments depend the whole Law and the Prophets" (Matthew 22:40). Imagine, the Law and the Prophets—thirty-nine books, hundreds of pages, thousands of lines, literally hundreds of thousands of words on life and living, on God and man, on family and friendship. The entire moral instruction from the mouth of God to the Old Testament people of God, captured in two great commandments. And at the heart of these two is one great directive—love.

Jesus also tells us that *love is the great authenticator,* demonstrating that our faith is real.

> "By this all men will know that you are My disciples, if you have love for one another." (John 13:35)

In the marketplace of goods and services, trademarks are prized and protected because they authenticate a product's manufacturer or the company providing a service. Knockoffs, on the other hand, not only cut into market share, they deprive customers of the quality they're expecting to get for their investment.

Similarly, while doctrines are important and creeds are crucial, when Jesus looks for a mark of authentication, a stamp guaranteeing genuine faith, He looks for love. That's the supreme symbol of true Christianity, and it's what we should be looking for too.

Finally, Jesus lets us know that *love is the great apologetic,* convincing the world that our message of love is indeed from God.

> "Sanctify them in the truth ... that they may all be one; even as You, Father, are in Me and I in You, that they may also be in Us, so that the world may believe that You sent Me." (John 17:17,21)

Every generation seems to have its prophets, preachers, and holy men declaring that they have "the truth." Jesus wasn't the first One to say, "Follow Me," and certainly isn't the last. The love He engenders in His followers, though, sets Him apart. That love proclaims that the founder of Christianity really is the Way, Truth, and Life. Great works by gallant defenders of the faith certainly have value, but Jesus said that the greatest apologetic, the strongest evidence for Christianity, is Christians who excel at loving.

Love is the great commandment, the great authenticator, and the great apologetic. And as we'll see when we begin to examine Paul's words to the Corinthian Christians, love is the great essential for all of life. Before turning the page to chapter 1, though, take a moment to savor the thirteenth chapter of the apostle's letter. Nothing written before or since Paul put pen to paper has described so clearly or beautifully the only brand of love that never fails. Savor each phrase as you read, then turn the page and join in our discovery of this magnificent love.

LOVE THAT NEVER FAILS

If I speak with the tongues of men and of angels, but do not have love,
I have become a noisy gong or a clanging cymbal.
If I have the gift of prophecy, and know all mysteries and all knowledge;
and if I have all faith, so as to remove mountains,
but do not have love, I am nothing.
And if I give all my possessions to feed the poor,
and if I surrender my body to be burned,
but do not have love, it profits me nothing.

Love is patient, love is kind and is not jealous;
love does not brag and is not arrogant,
does not act unbecomingly; it does not seek its own,
is not provoked, does not take into account a wrong suffered,
does not rejoice in unrighteousness, but rejoices with the truth;
bears all things, believes all things, hopes all things, endures all things

Love never fails;
but if there are gifts of prophecy, they will be done away;
If there are tongues, they will cease;
if there is knowledge, it will be done away.
For we know in part and we prophesy in part;
but when the perfect one comes, the partial will be done away.
When I was a child, I used to speak like a child,
think like a child, reason like a child;
when I became a man, I did away with childish things.
For now we see in a mirror dimly, but then face to face;
now I know in part, but then I will know fully
just as I also have been fully known.
But now faith, hope, love, abide these three;
but the greatest of these is love.

1 Corinthians 13

the priority
of LOVE

I once heard a rephrasing of the adage "keep first things first" that caught my attention and that serves as a great reminder to keep love on top of your life's to-do list. The words are Ken Poure's. He simply said, "Always keep the main thing . . . the main thing."

In this first section of his letter to the Corinthian church, Paul leaves no doubt that living without love is not an option. How important is this issue? Is it primary or secondary? He answers these questions emphatically. Love is to be the number one priority in your life. Don't be fooled into thinking that anything else can usurp its place of primacy. Love and love alone is to be the driving directive in your life and mine. And as we're about to see in these first three verses of 1 Corinthians 13, Paul makes a most convincing case for his conviction.

chapter one

Love:
Life's Great
Essential

Food, water, air . . . engine, brakes, suspension . . . readin', writin', and 'rithmetic . . . offense, defense, and special teams . . . hitting, pitching, fielding . . . roots, stems, leaves . . . fuel, heat, oxygen. What do these trios have in common? They represent the essentials of their respective fields of study or endeavor.

Webster defines the essentials as "constituting or part of the essence of something, basic or indispensable." Necessary. Fundamental. Vital. The "gotta have it" components of anything. Food, water, and air . . . the essentials for bodily life. The three Rs . . . the bedrock essentials of education. In the NFL, it's offense, defense, and special teams. For any baseball team competing at any level, it's hitting, pitching, and fielding.

When it comes to living, really living, God says there is just one essential: love. The apostle Paul took Jesus at His word. That's why the opening lines of his love letter, 1 Corinthians 13, make the point clear in the extreme. Love is the great essential, he says, the stuff life is made of. Learn to love and you learn to live. But if you lack love, nothing you do in life impresses God. You could sacrifice your life and you'd die in vain. So if you're serious about living, the starting point is to get serious about loving. You've got to realize that without love, you're dead before you start.

There are all kinds of ways to make a point. For this one, Paul chooses hyperbole. Extreme exaggeration. But this exaggeration is not intended to distort truth. It's intended to deliver it with a jolt. It's designed to wake up a sleeping soul. So how essential is love? Listen to Paul's words:

> If I speak with the tongues of men and of angels, but do not have love, I have become a noisy gong or a clanging cymbal. (v.1)

In other words, Paul says that if I could speak every language on earth—make that in heaven and on earth—but my words lacked love, I might as well save my breath. It doesn't matter how fluent I am in how many dialects or whether I am the ultimate communicator. *Without love I have nothing of value to say.* Nothing worth listening to. Nothing but noise.

In fact, whatever the language, words without love are more likely to hurt than help. Confront without love and someone gets hurt. Correct without love and someone gets hurt. Complain without love and someone gets hurt. Condemn without love and someone gets hurt. Console without love and someone who's already hurting gets hurt worse. In most cases, when love is missing from the communication, you lose—and so does the person on the receiving end.

It is necessary at this point to address an important issue. Some have taught that this verse is encouraging

Christians to seek and speak an angelic language. I don't believe so. Neither is it teaching that a person with the gift of tongues should be able to speak all human languages. Rather, it's as if Paul is employing progressive hyperbole to emphasize his point. It's as if he's saying, "Let's take things to the extreme. What if I could speak every language of every people group on the planet. Oh, you think that even though it sounds impossible, there might just be one person who could learn all those dialects? OK, let's really beef up the case. How about if I'm able to speak as the angels? That's right, even then, even if I could gab with Gabriel (which is impossible), without love my words would amount to nothing." Why? Because love is the great essential.

If this noisy-gong word picture wasn't loud and clear enough for his readers, Paul picked another one, equally extreme.

If I have the gift of prophecy, and know all mysteries and all knowledge... (v. 2a)

Here, again, is the power of hyperbole. Paul is not suggesting that the gift of prophecy gives a person "all knowledge" or unlocks "all mysteries." In fact, later in this very chapter he declares that we "know in part" until we are with the Savior. His point is not to define the gift of prophecy but to declare the absolute necessity of love, no matter how smart we may be. *Ultimate, even supernatural knowledge, without love, leaves us handicapped for real life.*

Life is built on *relationships*, not knowledge. This shouldn't surprise us. In the Creation account we read that God said, "Let Us make man in Our image, according to Our likeness." Relationship—the "Us" and the

"Our"—is clearly part of the triune Deity. So is it any wonder that after the Lord God created Adam, He quickly observed that "it is not good for the man to be alone"? The missing ingredient was relationship. Being created in God's image requires that we learn to love like God loves. To learn that lesson, Adam needed someone who was "bone of his bone and flesh of his flesh" to love.

This isn't to say that education is unimportant or knowledge is bad. Learning is essential, but without love, it cannot equip me for living, because life is built on relationships. How eloquently Paul put it when he wrote in another letter, this one to the Ephesian church, of his desire that they would "know the love of Christ which surpasses knowledge" (Ephesians 3:19). And Paul could not be implying that knowledge is bad. The same apostle wrote, "Study to shew thyself approved" (2 Timothy 2:15 KJV). Whether in our culture or his, such a premise would not only be *politically* incorrect, but also *biblically* incorrect. Check out Solomon's proverbs. One of the reasons he wrote them was "to give . . . youth knowledge and discretion" (Proverbs 1:4). What Paul was saying was that knowledge is not enough. Without love, it is —well, you guessed it—*nothing*.

The picture was getting clearer, but Paul wasn't through making his point.

> If I have all faith, so as to move mountains, but do not have love, I am nothing. (v. 2b)

At this point it is appropriate to point out what a wise scholar once told me. "In the Greek," he said, "*nothing* means 'nothing.'" So if you think that boosting your spirituality will somehow put you on the road to a more fulfilling life, but you leave love back in the garage, you're going absolutely nowhere. *Ultimate spirituality without love is of no value.* Period. It doesn't matter if you have enough faith to say, "You know, Lord, I'd really like a view of the mountains. So, Lord, I'm asking that you move one of the Rocky Mountains next to my home here in Southern California. Amen." Suddenly you heard a rumble. The earth shook, and as you opened your eyes, presto! The Rockies were outside your window. Even if you had the faith to relocate the ski slopes of Vail and the beaches of Florida and the forests of New England to the deserts of Nevada to create your own paradise, your spirituality would be of no value to God.

By now the picture was just about as clear as crystal, but Paul wasn't taking any chances. He got absolutely graphic to drive the point home with one more hyperbole.

> *If I give all my possessions to feed the poor, and if I surrender my body to be burned, but do not have love, it profits me nothing. (v. 3)*

Surely sacrifice—make that the ultimate sacrifice—will win me a hearing in heaven. After all, what could count more than giving my very life? All I own . . . no, let's take this sacrifice a step further. I'll give all I own *and then* offer my very body as a sacrifice, but not just any sacrifice. Let me suffer by being burned at the stake for my faith or for my friends. Now won't that win a hearing with God?

At this point, I'm sure Paul would hope, the answer comes quickly. "No way!" God's not interested in our sacrifices. He declared that repeatedly through His prophets. *A sacrifice of "love" is what God longs for.* It doesn't matter to Him whether I give 10 percent of my goods to the church. Or 50 percent. Or even 90 percent. Maybe I decide to give every dime I make for the rest of my life to God's work. If I'm not giving love, God is not impressed. On the contrary, He is grieved. "Go and learn what this means," Jesus told the Pharisees, "'I desire compassion, and not sacrifice'" (Matthew 9:13).

See why love is the great essential? Because with it, while we may not be able to do all things, what we can do counts for eternity. We're able to live as God intended, not for ourselves, but in relationship with Him and with the people He puts in our lives, just as the Great Commandment says: Love God and love people. Love is life's *great essential*.

GODLY LOVE IS SERVANT LOVE

Now, we're beginning to understand the ground rules for loving God's way, but if we're serious about learning to love like He loves, we need to come to grips with one more critical component of divine love before we begin. Godly love is servant love. It's other-centered. We'll explore this idea more fully in chapter 6, but from the start we need to keep it out in the open and remind ourselves often that it's there. To make the point, turn again to Paul's letter to the Philippians. Keep John 3:16 in mind as you read these words:

> Have this attitude in yourselves which was also in Christ Jesus, who, although He existed in the form of God, did not regard equality with God a thing to be grasped, but emptied Himself, taking the form of a bond-servant. (Philippians 2:5–7)

Jesus' example leaves no doubt: loving means serving, sacrificially if necessary. There's that word again: *sacrifice*. But this time it's held up as a model of ultimate

love. Love that gives . . . love that pays a price, gets people's attention. Our church family in Fullerton sees the
impact sacrificial love can have on a watching world
every year when we send teams of people around the
world for short-term missions projects. In the summer
of 1997 my older daughter, Beth, and two dozen other
high school seniors "sacrificed" their summer to go on
one of these projects. After a ten-day training camp in
the States, these kids spent six weeks building an evan-
gelical church in a small city in Poland. They dug dirt,
mixed mortar and concrete, tied rebar, laid bricks, took
turns on KP duty. They also memorized Scripture, took
turns leading daily devotions, and studied the Bible together.

When the kids weren't building, studying, or doing
laundry (by hand in tubs), they were often walking the
streets in small towns, looking for opportunities to meet
people, explain why they had come, and share their
faith. People were often shocked to find that these
teenaged Americans had not only given up their summer vacations to help a struggling church, but that they
had also raised money and paid their own way to come
and do the work. That's sacrifice! Sacrificial love gets
people's attention.

Even in difficult times—or maybe we should say especially in difficult times—Jesus' brand of love attracts
people to Him. Continuing in his letter to the Philippians, Paul described the ultimate response to Jesus' sacrifice:

> *Therefore also God highly exalted Him ... that at the name of Jesus,
> every knee should bow, ... and that every tongue will confess, that Je-
> sus Christ is Lord. (Philippians 2:9–11)*

I saw the magnetic affect of a Christlike response to tragedy illustrated at my former church not long ago during what turned out to be a good news/bad news weekend. The good news was that the church had a resounding 99 percent vote to call a candidate as their new senior pastor. Almost two years after my departure, they had found a godly man to come and lead them. It was a time of relieved rejoicing.

That same weekend, though, which happened to be Father's Day weekend, turned to tragedy for Joy and Mike, a wonderful young couple in the church. They live just inside the city limits, about a mile from the nearest grocery store. Joy planned to make Father's Day memorable for Mike, and on Saturday evening she thought of one final touch to make his day extraspecial. Flowers. So she hopped in the car for that short drive to the store. A five-minute trip tops. On the way home, though, she met a sixteen-year-old kid who had just gotten his driver's license and decided to go out drinking with his buddies to celebrate. They met head-on as the teenager's car crossed the center line and struck Joy's vehicle.

The next day, as Joy lay in a coma, the church gathered around Mike and their two little boys, ages five and seven. Joy lived a few days, into the following week, but she never regained consciousness. Then, suddenly, she was gone. Now you've got a young dad with two kids . . . and no wife. That's when love went into action. The church family began to pour out incredible support, comfort, and practical help. In the midst of terrible grief, faith came to the front, and love ushered it in.

I did a lot of funerals in my years at that church, but never one that was packed out. This one was standing room only. My former associate officiated, and he said there were people all around the room he'd never seen before. "Not just our people," he said. "People from all around the community." People like one lady who called and said, "I don't go to church, but I was so impressed with all the love I saw your people showing for one another around this family that I want to know when the services are. I want to come see what's going on. I think I need that."

That's the power of God's love. In the midst of a tragic death it can spark new life. In the midst of deep grief it can restore joy. Jesus said, "By this all men will know that you are My disciples, if you have love for one another" (John 13:35). It is the Bible's *great commandment,* the gospel's *great apologetic,* and the Christian's defining *mark of authenticity.* When real people see the contrast between a life simply focused on self and a life constructed around servant love, it sometimes grabs their attention in a way that won't let go. They yearn to understand how real love by real people in the real world really works. That's what I want. How about you?

The apostle Paul knew that this divine love had to be defined in extremely practical terms. People needed a definition anyone could understand and put into operation in everyday life. So Paul delivered. He spends the rest of his epistle on love drawing out the detailed description we're looking for: a job description for people who want to go to work as full-time lovers. Let's read on and see what he has to say.

part two

the profile
of LOVE

Right about now you may be saying to yourself, "OK, Paul, I get the picture. Love is to be the driving priority in my life. And I'm convinced that it's essential if I'm ever going to live life God's way. But how do I get there from here? For starters, I'm not sure I understand what you mean when you say love. *And besides, even if I did understand, how in the world could I hope to pull it off?"*

This kind of reaction to Paul's words shouldn't surprise you. At least not if you've grown up in the twentieth century . . . or read the works of earlier authors or thinkers. To some, love is a pit you fall into. To others, it's a sweet dream you hope never ends. For some, it's a feeling you've never had before, and for others, it's like a disease you catch. Some think it's sex in the backseat of a Chevy; others see it as a never-ending journey. When I was first starting to date, I asked a pastor friend, who shall remain anonymous, "How will I know when it's the real thing?" His reply: "You'll just know," quieted my fears for the moment, but the first time I put them to the test, they left me wondering, "What kind of an answer was that?"

I can't hold it against him, though. Listen to what these "wise" men and women had to say about love.

Love is merely a madness; and, I tell you, deserves as well a dark house and a whip as madmen do; and the reason

*why they are not so punish'd and cured is, that the lunacy
is so ordinary, that the whippers are in love too.*
—Shakespeare

To love is virtually to know; to know is not virtually to love.
—Anonymous

Of course, not everyone has fallen this short of the mark in
his quest to define true love. One songwriter called love "a
many-splendored thing," and it is certainly that. I once heard it
said that "love is a load—and blessed is he who bears a heavy
one." Again, these are wise words. No one, though, has tackled
the assignment of defining love with such inspired wisdom as
Paul, nor was anyone so successful at coming up with practical definitions and sound advice. The next four verses of 1 Corinthians 13 will take anyone who is serious about loving into
the tough terrain of true love and bring him or her out again
better equipped to continue the climb.

chapter two

Love Is Patient and Kind

LOVE IS PATIENT

Society has a lot to say about patience these days, but the hard truth is it's in frighteningly short supply. Just take a look at the stands during a little league game. Or check out the face of that person you just edged out of the only vacant parking spot at the mall on Christmas Eve. Or check your blood pressure next time you're on a crowded plane in the seat just ahead of a screaming three-year-old. The most unsettling indicator of a patience shortage, though, turned up in the news recently. "Road rage" has been identified as a leading cause of fatal automobile accidents.

That gives a whole new twist to the term "defensive driving," doesn't it? So what's the answer? Ride a bike or take a bus? No, what we need is not another mode of transportation. Whether it's on the highway or in the home, when things start to heat up, what we need is *transformation*. We need the kind of radical change of heart that produces radically different behavior. "God is love," and "love is patient," and by God's grace, when His Spirit comes to live in us, patience moves in too. Our challenge is to see that same patience bubble to the surface as a gift from God that we get to share with those He loves.

The word that we read as "patience" in the text is *makrothumeo*, which is a fascinating combination of Greek terms. *Makro* means far or long; *thumeo* means heat, such as we see in words like *thermos* or *thermometer*. Paul's idea of patience is to hang in, to persevere, to remain under the heat. James (5:7) compares patience to a farmer who works faithfully while waiting for the fruit of his labor to break through the soil and reach maturity.

> *Be patient, therefore, brethren, until the coming of the Lord. Behold, the farmer waits for the precious produce of the soil, being patient about it, until it gets the early and late rains. You too be patient; strengthen your hearts, for the coming of the Lord is at hand. (James 5:7–8)*

Farming involves a lot of hard work—plowing and planting, weeding and fertilizing. Then, before you hardly turn around, there are more weeds to hoe, rows to disk and insects to spray. Farming is down and dirty work, and at the end of the week, what does the farmer have to show for all those early mornings and long hours in the field? Acres and acres of dirt. Rearranged and overworked dirt. That's it! And a man can't feed a family on dirt!

That's why every successful farmer needs at least as much patience as perspiration. Waiting becomes as important, and sometimes as difficult, as working. Patience is the work of love that waits. The farmer does all he can do to produce the desired crop, and then he waits. He knows it's now up to God to bring the rains, sprout new growth, and produce the fruit of harvest. And if he's experienced, he's learned that sitting by the field in a lawn chair doesn't make it come any sooner. So he goes about his other business, trusting that in time the crop will indeed sprout and grow. Then all his hard work will pay off. But first, he must give the seeds he planted time to change, mature, and bear fruit. That willingness to wait is at the heart of patience.

Now you may be thinking, "Hey, the farming analogy is quaint, but I'm not dealing with corn here, I'm dealing with kids. I'm not dealing with wheat, I'm dealing with a wife. And they just need to pick up the pace more times than I care to count." Whether it's farming or family or friends, the point is the same. Patience is a waiting game, and how we wait makes all the difference.

Try this definition:

patience · love that waits with contentment

What does that involve? It means I wait without demanding change. I wait without anxiety. I wait without anger. Patience is more than either an attitude or an action. *It's action with an attitude.* You see, it's possible for me to be waiting and waiting and waiting on you. That's perseverance, and perseverance is good. But if my attitude's wrong, there's no patience. Stubbornness, yes, but not patience. Which means there's no love either. Perseverance is the action, but patience infuses that action with an attitude of contentment or peace.

If the farming analogy fell flat for you, maybe fishing is your thing. One writer said that patience is faith waiting for a nibble. I can relate to that. If I'm sitting in my little fishing boat and I have faith that there are really some keepers below the waterline, I'll sit under that hot summer sun all day long waiting for one to bite. It's when my faith falters that I give up hope and head for home. Or I bend the rules.

Like the time a college buddy and I went fishing for some famous West Virginia "golden trout," a hybrid first developed in that part of the country. Believe it or not, we came across a shallow pool at the edge of the stream that was sealed off from the rest of the river. And sitting right in center of that pool was the biggest golden trout we'd seen all day. Well, we baited our hooks in a hurry and laid them in front of that fish. But instead of striking, he ignored the temptation. No matter what we dangled in front of his nose, this fish was not going to go for it. Did we wait patiently until he got around to taking the bait? Nope. My buddy and I picked up a couple of big rocks and on the count of three heaved them in the vicinity of Mr. Aloof. The strategy worked. The fish was stunned, and we netted him before he came to. Unfortunately, it's illegal to "rock" a fish in West Virginia. Score one for impatience.

Another way to look at patience is to think about its opposite. What's the antithesis of a patient spirit? I'd say a nagging spirit. *Nag.* Now there's a word with some bite to it. *Naaag.* Sounds like what it means, doesn't it? Webster calls that onomatopoeia. Proverbs says, "Better to live in the corner of the house-top than have a nagging wife and a brawling household" (Proverbs 25:24 NEB). Now if you're a guy, don't go getting an attitude here. Proverbs also says to beware of the dangers of a contentious or nagging man (Proverbs 26:21). Man or woman, we all have the tendency to nag, which simply means to push someone. Proverbs also compares nagging to the dripping of water on a windowsill on a rainy day. Drip. Drip. Drip. Drip. It may be small, but it's constant. It never lets up.

If I have a patient spirit, though, I do let up. I'm willing to wait on you, to keep from bugging you. And why do we bug people, push them, nag them? Last time I caught myself pushing my wife, Becky, I realized the issue was simply that I wasn't willing to trust God with Becky's timetable. You see, if patience is a gift of love, I'm giving my wife the freedom to stay on her timetable. I'm giving the kids freedom to stay on their timetable. And I'm trusting God to meet my needs even while they may be running behind my schedule.

Now don't get impatient with me here. I'm not saying that schedules aren't important or that deadlines don't matter. But I am saying that, more times than we care to admit, *our impatience is much more a matter of selfishness than timeliness*. And in those situations, if I'm not able to trust God to meet my needs, how do I respond? I get pushy. I take over the situation. Maybe what I need to do is pray, but I don't because I'm too busy lighting a fire under everybody, turning up the heat rather than persevering under the heat with a spirit of contentment.

The upshot of this approach is the uncomfortable realization that *patience is a faith issue*. My capacity to be patient is in direct proportion to my faith in God. If I really believe that He can meet my needs when others are not meeting them, then I can be patient to wait for people to change. I can be patient at my job to hang in there under less than ideal circumstances . . . and do so with a joyful spirit. I can be patient with a friend who doesn't respond to a request when and how I wish he would. I can be patient with the kids when they slam the front door for the fifth time despite my repeated reminders that it latches just as well if closed gently. This kind of patience allows us to love slow-to-change people and give them the gift of time.

Patience of this sort flows most often from someone with a servant's heart. A good, practical example would be the waiter at our favorite restaurant. To get an idea of what we're *not* talking about here, imagine this scene. My wife Becky and I are sitting at a quiet table in the corner, looking forward to an unhurried dinner and conversation. Trouble is, throughout the meal, every time the waiter comes by he's checking his watch. And just as we're taking the last few bites of dinner and are almost ready for a cup of coffee, he stops to say, "You know, you've really been here a long time. You ought to be finishing up so someone else can have this table. I mean, you've had enough time to eat that. Here, let me take your plate, and I'll bring you the bill."

Sounds ludicrous, doesn't it? That's because it's the antithesis of what we've been talking about. If you're a genuine servant, you'll let me sit there all night long and drink fifty cups of coffee with my wife. The last thing you want to do is make me feel hurried or rushed.

Patience is a hallmark of servant love—and "patience" that lacks a servant's attitude is not patience at all. Love is patient. Patience is a waiting game, and how we wait makes all the difference.

LOVE IS KIND

Paul links patience and kindness for good reason. Just as two candles shed more light than one in the darkness, so patience and kindness together tend to speak the message of love more forcefully, without words.

Kindness has been called the only universal language. Even those who cannot communicate verbally can speak it, and those who are hearing impaired can hear and understand it. The reason is simple. Kindness is first and foremost an action. It is love expressed by what we do.

The Greek word translated here as "kind," *chresteuomai*, is only used this one time in the New Testament, but the family of words related to it help us understand why it was selected as an attribute of love. The primary root from which it springs (think of it as the great-grandfather of our word), is *chrao*, which means "to lend or to furnish what is needed." One noun, *chrema*, its linguistic first cousin, if you will, means "a thing which one needs." It is translated in the gospels and Acts (see Acts 4:37) as "money" or "wealth." Now we are getting practical. To borrow from an adage, kindness puts its money where its mouth is. It pays the price to meet the need. Hence a common definition is "to act benevolently or to be found useful." From studying these terms, we can better understand what's at the root of kindness. The common "DNA" found in this family of words is helpfulness, usefulness, a tendency to see a need and meet it.

Its closest relative (think of it as a brother) is "kindness," which is translated as "easy" in Matthew 11:30, where Jesus says, "My yoke is easy and My burden is light." Isn't that interesting? He's saying, "My yoke is kind. It's not burdensome to you. On the contrary, it's helpful, useful."

Let's try this for a definition of kindness:

kindness · love that initiates to help meet a need

Think of it this way. Let's say you and your family or friends are running late for a night at the ballpark. You know—hot dogs, peanuts, foul balls during batting practice. You're eager to take in the whole experience, but getting all the stuff together for the game—baseball mitts, stadium chairs, caps, sunglasses—is taking longer than you would have hoped or expected. Now, instead of saying, "Hey, are you about ready? I'd like to get there before my clothes go out of style," kindness asks, "What can I do to help us get ready faster?"

Once again, that servant attitude shines through. Servants notice needs and respond to them. As with patience, both attitude and action are involved. Kindness can take a thousand different forms, but in every one of them it always takes the initiative to help.

You may have heard of a popular book entitled *Conspiracy of Kindness,* by Steve Sjogren.[1] It speaks of one church's successful use of what they call "random acts of kindness" in their community to attract people to the gospel message. It shouldn't surprise us that this approach works. Anytime we take the initiative to help someone else, especially when he least expects it, he has to take notice, and usually the reaction is positive.

A friend of mine had an experience recently that proves the point. He had sprained his knee rather severely and had to wear a full-leg immobilizer for a while. He was still hobbled with that device when he flew out of town for a family vacation. And wouldn't you know, the jetway at the gate was out of commission, so all the passengers, including my friend, had to walk down a set of stairs, across the tarmac, and up another set of stairs into the plane. As it turned out, the leg brace, while awkward, wasn't as much of a hassle as trying to haul an armload of carry-on materials while negotiating the stairway. But just as my friend was feeling a bit self-conscious for his slow progress, an airline employee slipped up behind him, whisked the stuff out from under his arm, and hustled it out to the plane. They met again at the foot of the stairs by the plane, and the airline guy simply smiled, said the stuff was just inside the entrance, and trotted off to do his job.

That's kindness. Taking the initiative to meet a need. And if our love is characterized by similar actions, it is true love indeed.

If the airline guy's random act of kindness makes the point, another guy's behavior under much more serious circumstances drives it home. This incident also occurred during a trip. One traveler was surprised by hooligans who beat him senseless, took his valuables, and left him for dead. The first two passersby, churchmen no less, could have helped him, but neither did. I hope they had their reasons, but instead of taking the initiative, they not only turned a blind eye to the victim's plight, they headed to the other side of the street so they wouldn't even have to look at him. The next guy to come along, though, was different . . .

> A Samaritan, as he traveled, came where the man was; and when he saw him, he took pity on him. He went to him and bandaged his wounds, pouring on oil and wine. Then he put the man on his own donkey, took him to an inn and took care of him. The next day he took out two silver coins and gave them to the innkeeper. "Look after him," he said, "and when I return, I will reimburse you for any extra expense you may have." (Luke 10:33–35 NIV)

You probably know that it was Jesus who first recounted this story . . . to a group of people who couldn't quite get it when He tried to explain true love to them. And do you remember what He said when He finished the story?

"Go and do likewise."

That was a classic random act of kindness, and it's our best model for communicating love to a hurting world. I've found that love expressed this way is most effective when it's least expected. So keep surprise on your side. Think of it as "ambushing" someone with love. Mugging them with loving-kindness. Muggers strike quickly, while their victims' defenses are down. Hit people with kindness at times like that and you'll definitely get their attention.

To get the idea, picture this scene. You're lingering in the family room after dinner and you spot your spouse going to work on the dirty dishes. Just as your attention is being drawn back to the television, the phone rings. You answer with a fatigued, "Hello," then, "Oh, yes, just a minute. Honey, it's for you." You hand off the phone, but instead of flopping back down on the couch, you get a burst of inspiration and strike, moving swiftly to the sink and doing the dishes. Just as you finish you hear the phone conversation end and your spouse returns to the kitchen, but it's too late. The dishes are clean. You've mugged the one you love!

NOTE

1. Steve Sjogren, *Conspiracy of Kindness* (Ann Arbor, Mich.: Vine Books, Servant, 1993).

chapter three

Love Is Not Jealous or Envious

LOVE IS NOT JEALOUS

When Solomon wrote of jealousy centuries before the apostle Paul penned this letter, he acknowledged its power over men and women and used powerful imagery to make his point. "Jealousy," said the wisest of men, "is cruel as the grave" (Song of Solomon 8:6 KJV). Just as jealousy has brought down kings and kingdoms, queens and countries, so it is the death knell to relationships when left unchecked. When love longs to breathe freely, jealousy chokes it.

Is it any wonder the Lord God prescribed a "law of jealousy" to help men contend with this monster of an emotion, which He called "the spirit of jealousy" (Numbers 5)? Or that the psalmist and Ezekiel both refer to divine jealousy as a fiery emotion? Or that in his proverbs Solomon warns that in making another man jealous you will not only enrage him but, worse yet, you'll be ill-equipped to appease his anger? We're obviously playing with fire here, and the clear message of those in the know is that all who play stand to get burned. That would explain why the Hebrews had only one word for jealousy in the Old Testament—*qua-nah*. It means to be intensely red.

The Greek word Paul uses is similar, *zeloō*, usually translated with terms like envy, covet, desire, or be zealous. Its linguistic grandfather is a verb that means "to boil or to be hot." In the book of James we are warned that the heat of jealousy or envy can ignite conflict and leave some nasty scars.

> *You lust and do not have; so you commit murder. And you are envious [zeloo] and cannot obtain; so you fight and quarrel. (James 4:2)*

At the root of jealousy is a burning desire to have what I cannot or do not have. And if I can't get it one way, I'll try another and another and another until I get what I want. If I have to go to war, so be it. It's all about possession and control. But it's a classic case of winning a battle but losing the war. The jealous husband or wife may win control in the short run, but a spirit of mistrust and jealousy will do little to endear "the possessed" to the "possessor." People are not possessions to be owned, put in their place, and controlled. Love doesn't seek to control; it trusts and grants freedom.

I learned the hard way what getting burned by jealousy means when I headed off to college. My wife Becky and I were dating when I graduated from high school. I was two years older, though, so when I went away to school our relationship had to be maintained long-distance. I'd come home on weekends, but since this was in pre-E-mail days, during the week we had to rely on letters to stay in touch. From the start, I struggled with that age-old "spirit of jealousy."

The simple truth, of course, was that I had no reason to be jealous. Although our relationship was relatively new, we were dating seriously, and Becky took our relationship to heart. She loved me. But here I was, away at college, and there she was, this good-looking young lady, back home. She was president of the student body her senior year and was runner-up to the homecoming queen, and she'd die if she knew I was telling you all this.

On one particular occasion when I came home for the weekend, my thoughts ran away from me. As a candidate for homecoming queen, Becky had to be escorted onto the football field at halftime of the big game by a member of her class. I clearly remember sitting in the football stands, fuming, watching this guy walk her onto the field. There she was, my sweetheart, looking her beautiful sweet self, sitting next to this other guy on the backseat of a shiny convertible as they were delivered to the home team's sideline, right in front of the stands filled with hundreds of people. There she was, holding his arm as they walked to midfield. And there I sat, in the stands, by myself. Fuming.

I was jealous. Being the class act she was (and still is), Becky wasn't impressed with my jealousy. Fact is, it frustrated her, because it was undeniable evidence that I didn't trust her. William Shakespeare said that jealousy "is the green-ey'd monster which doth mock the meat it feeds on." Another author wrote that it's the great exaggerator. It sees things that aren't even there. That was my problem. There was nothing there, but my lack of trust fabricated a monster. Drawing from that experience, here's what I see as a good working definition for Paul's challenge to love by not being jealous:

not jealous • love that trusts instead of controls

Choosing to trust builds a love relationship. Choosing to trust keeps that love relationship strong. And choosing to trust is how you keep from losing that which you cherish. On the other hand, it has been accurately observed that jealousy is the best way to get rid of what you're afraid of losing. *Jealousy drives people away. It fuels the inclination to flee.* If you're struggling right now in a relationship with someone you love, perhaps your spouse, who is tempted to leave, your acting jealous is all the evidence that person needs to justify the decision to walk away. Jealousy always drives people away; it never draws them back, because it says, "I don't trust you." And love relationships have to be built on trust.

With close to 60 percent of marriages ending in divorce these days, most of us are personally and painfully acquainted with people whose "till death us do part" has disappeared in the quicksand of broken promises. One thing this tragic reality tells us is that millions of people, both injured spouses and children who are hurt by the fallout from broken marriages, now have greater difficulty trusting others. In the face of such pain, love that is not jealous does not come easily, but by God's grace, it can come.

Statistics are impossible to compile on the number of marriages that remain intact but have been damaged by a violation of trust. In these cases, the wife or husband whose spouse has been unfaithful will understandably grapple with jealousy, even if the errant partner has sought forgiveness and reconciliation. "How do I know he won't do it again?" or "How can I trust her around other men now?" are legitimate cries of a wounded mate. The tendency is then to demand moment-by-moment accountability, to pull on the reins of control, to question or interrogate every time the violator leaves early or arrives home late. The danger is that such control will choke off efforts to restore the relationship.

When working with couples who are trying to reconcile after such a devastating blow, I tell them that they must eventually choose to trust instead of seeking control. Such undeserved confidence and love carry an alluring message of hope. No amount of fencing in can stop spouses from second affairs. They will eventually find a time and a place. But *love given freely, love that is not forced, has the power to heal broken relationships.* A rocky relationship romanced with the gift of freedom is far more likely to recover than a relationship repelled by a jealous spirit.

Of course marriages aren't the only love relationships that get burned by jealousy. Family relationships, friendships, professional relationships—all are susceptible to this fire hazard. I like the way Chuck Swindoll explained the dangers of jealousy.

> Here is the way it works. I love something very much, indeed, too much. I pursue it with zeal. I desire, in fact, to possess it completely. But the thing I love passes out of my hands and into another's. I begin to experience the gnawing pangs of jealousy. Strangely, the feelings of zeal and love begin to change. By the dark, transforming power of sin, my love turns to hate. Once I was open, happy, filled to the brim with exquisite delight, but no longer! Now I am closed within a narrow compass of inner rage, intensely and insanely angry.[1]

LOVE IS NOT ENVIOUS

When Paul wrote that love is not jealous, it's possible that he had something else, or something more than mere jealousy, in mind. The Greek term he used can also mean "envious." In fact, when the *New International Version* translates this passage it says, "Love does not . . . envy." This is similar to not being jealous in two ways. First, it involves a choice. Second, it brings freedom.

When I reject jealousy, I choose to trust another person. When I reject envy, I choose to trust God. I'm no longer worrying about what I do or don't have. I'm content. Rather than envying what others possess, I trust God to bless me as He wishes and when He wishes. So now I appreciate my job rather than compare it to someone else's. I'm thankful for a friendship rather than envious of others' relationships. I'm content with the potential and gifts in my children instead of comparing them to their peers. I'm content with and appreciative of my wife or husband instead of always comparing her to the woman down the street or him to the guy down the pew or someone down the hall.

Great freedom comes when love chooses to remove envy from the equation, because suddenly I'm free to celebrate not only my successes but also the successes of others. By not worrying about when or how God blesses my spouse or my friend or my boss or a coworker, I am free to "rejoice with those who rejoice" and more fully love each of those people. This kind of love, love without envy, builds, whereas envy destroys. All that envy builds is barriers between me and those I might love. By rejecting envy, I'm free to both love and be loved. Try this out for a working definition:

not envious • love that trusts God and is content with what He gives

If we're deliberate about nurturing an attitude of gratitude to God for His countless blessings and matchless grace, envy will find little room to rampage in our hearts. Contentment will squeeze it out every time. And when we're content, we're far more inclined to speak and act lovingly.

What does raw envy sound like and look like? Remember the impatient waiter we met in the previous chapter? The guy who kept rushing us through dinner? If that waiter also suffered from a bad case of the envys, couldn't you picture him delivering our meal with a comment like, "Here's your dinner. You don't really deserve to eat here. Not like I do. I've been working here for over five years and have catered to more people than you can count. And tonight I've been going in and out of that kitchen door for the last six hours fetching food for people the chef doesn't even know. Well, now I'm hungry. It ought to be my turn to get served. Yeah, I wish I were eating this meal instead of you, but I'm not. So, well, here's your food."

You know a waiter with that attitude wouldn't last long. Inject a servant attitude into this situation, though, and everything changes. Suddenly, not only is the waiter excited to be serving a meal in this fine restaurant, but he's also free to enjoy with you or me the fact that we're having a good time as a result of his service. He enters into the joy of the party even though it's not for him.

There's that concept again: *serving*. When love has you and me serving, we don't have the time or the inclination to be jealous or envious. "Do not merely look out for your own personal interests, but also for the interests of others," Paul told the Philippians (Philippians 2:4), because he knew that selflessness is to relationships what "weed and feed" is to gardening. It helps plants or grass grow stronger and healthier, and it keeps the weeds away. Jealousy and envy are weeds of the worst kind. They choke the life—and the love—out of relationships. So whenever you find them springing up between you and the people you love (and they will keep springing up), you've only got one good option.

Dig them up and throw them away.

NOTE

1. Charles R. Swindoll, *Killing Giants, Pulling Thorns* (Grand Rapids: Zondervan, 1994), 29–30.

chapter four

Love Does Not Brag, Is Not Arrogant

LOVE DOES NOT BRAG

If you grew up in the 1960s, certain sounds and images and people and places are probably on permanent deposit in your memory banks. Filed under "social issues," you'll likely find a recollection of the Civil Rights movement. If it's "presidents," John F. Kennedy's assassination is right there. For "foreign affairs," there's the Vietnam War. Think "rock and roll" and the Beatles come to mind. The "movies" category includes *Bullet*, and "books" definitely has a slot for *The Ugly American*. "Football" conjures up Vince Lombardi's Green Bay Packers, "television" flashes *Star Trek* across your mental screen, and packed with everything else in the "California" category, just after the Beach Boys, is undoubtedly Berkeley in all its countercultural color.

Let's try one more. The section is "sports," subsection "boxing." Who do you think of first? Cassius Clay, right? Muhammad Ali. Was there any other boxer during that decade? And what do you recall of this prominent pugilist? Of course, that line he shouted to hype every upcoming bout: "I am the greatest! Ali is the greatest!" Muhammad Ali epitomized what Paul minimized. "Love does not brag," Paul wrote in the second half of verse 4, "and is not arrogant." Now in all fairness, there's no incongruity in Ali's bravado. His bragging and arrogance reflected no less love for his opponents than did his treatment of them in the ring.

When it comes to relationships, arrogance may win a battle, but it will never make you a champion lover. And if you're serious about going the distance in relationships, the attitude of arrogance that's reflected in boastful language will never win you points with the judges either—the significant people in your life—much less with the ultimate Judge. Servant-hearted lovers simply aren't into arrogance.

Let's deal with the symptom first, as Paul does: *bragging*. Then we'll address the disease behind it: *arrogance*. Bragging is an action that reflects an attitude of arrogance.

The Greek term *perpereuomai* appears only one time in all the New Testament. But it's related to the verb "to boast" and the noun for "braggart." It doesn't take a Greek scholar to see a pattern. When this person speaks, more often than not the sentence starts with "I." And what follows that shortest of pronouns is often a long string of accolades and accomplishments, quips and quotes, all designed to elevate the one speaking onto his own self-made pedestal.

It is a self-centered action, which by definition is quite unlike the actions of loving servants. An appropriate opposite action makes a good definition for this term:

not brag • love that speaks of others more than oneself

We've all known world-class braggarts. No matter what the topic, they're experts. No matter what the experience, they've done it. No matter what the issue, they have the final word. Do you feel loved as they ramble on and on about themselves? By contrast, world-class lovers redirect the attention to their beloved. Love elevates and celebrates the character and accomplishments of others. As a result, those who love by not bragging never lack for friends. Is it any wonder why?

When you're serious about being other-centered, you're genuinely interested in what those you love are thinking and feeling. Since thoughts and feelings are expressed through words, you discover what's on people's minds and hearts by listening to what they have to say. That means making room in your conversations and your time together for your loved one to speak. It also means creating an atmosphere in your relationship that invites honest and intimate communication. And at times it means biting your tongue or saving a comment for later or simply being courteous enough to let the other person finish expressing a thought before you chime in with one.

Think of the people you're most comfortable being with. What creates that ease of being together? Chances are the open communication between you has a lot to do with it, along with the lack of any need to impress. Conversation isn't a tool used to jockey for position in the relationship; it's a resource for getting you on an equal footing. And when communicating at this level, you usually find yourself talking about the other person. When this happens, love takes over and a sweet irony often kicks in. Namely, you essentially start bragging . . . about the other person.

One of the greatest ways to freshen up a marriage,

for example, is to brag on the strengths of your husband or wife. Not in an artificial or condescending way, but as the natural expression of your love. Let's face it, when someone builds you up publicly, despite the initial awkwardness, it makes you feel great inside. As much as we're inclined toward humility, we like it when someone compliments us in front of others.

The flip side of this aspect of human nature is that *love doesn't criticize a loved one publicly*. Whether it's friends or children, wife or husband, critical words spoken in front of others are like sulfuric acid on a relationship. They eat away at it. Brag on someone, though, and the opposite happens. Restoration occurs. Wounds are healed. Scars disappear. That's love's goal.

Sometimes our thoughts and feelings for other people fall right in line with what we're talking about here. We feel deep affection for them. We think highly of them. We appreciate them. We look up to them. Every thought of these people is a positive one. We could brag on them all day. The only problem is, they never know it. Whether due to procrastination ("I've *got* to let so-and-so know how much he means to me") or simply never getting around to it, we fail to express what we think and feel. If you've been guilty of this sort of negligence, maybe a little poem I heard recently will spur you to speak up.

SAY IT NOW

If with pleasure you are viewing, any work a man is doing,
If you like him or you love him, tell him now.
Don't withhold your approbation
    'til the parson makes oration,
And he lies with snowy lilies on his brow.
For no matter how you shout it, he won't really care about it.
He won't know how many teardrops you have shed.

If you think some praise is due him,
    now's the time to slip it to him,
For he cannot read his tombstone when he's dead.

More than fame, more than money,
    is the moment warm and sunny,
And the hearty, kind approval of a friend.
For it gives to life a savor, and it makes you stronger, braver.
And it gives strength and courage to the end.
If he earns your praise, bestow it.
If you like him, let him know it.

Let a word of true encouragement be said.
Do not wait 'till life is over, and he lies beneath the clover,
Because he cannot read his tombstone when he's dead.

It's pretty hard to brag when you're passing along well-deserved words of praise to those you love. Don't wait until it's too late for the object of your praise to profit from your eulogy. Brag on them now.

LOVE IS NOT ARROGANT

Now on to arrogance, the attitude behind the words of the boaster. Attitudes are almost always at the root of our actions, and bragging is no exception. When arrogance shows up, love soon disappears. Arrogance and its companion, Prideful, have an overinflated sense of their own importance. They demand to be the center of attention. They are puffed up with pride. In fact, the Greek word literally means "to puff up or blow up." The same root word surfaces in the noun for a bellows used to fan a fire. In this word picture, we find our definition for love that is not arrogant:

not arrogant · love that stays humble and inflates others instead of itself

First, love free of arrogance stays humble. A spirit of humility is the inverse of arrogance. People who stay humble, no matter what measure of success they attain or position of power they hold, can be potent lovers of others. Humility surfaces repeatedly as we explore the various aspects of love in 1 Corinthians 13. Let me illustrate:

The humble can wait patiently,
    while the arrogant wants it now!
The humble demonstrates kindness,
    while the arrogant doesn't even notice the need.
The humble are content, not jealous or envious,
    while the arrogant feel they deserve more.
The humble honors and esteems the other,
    while the arrogant brags on himself.
The humble does not act unbecomingly,
    while the arrogant's manners are rude.
The humble shows a servant spirit,
    while the arrogant demands to be served.
The humble are not easily provoked,
    while the arrogant are quick to take offense.
The humble quickly forgive a wrong suffered,
    while the arrogant can't rest until they even the score.

Get the point? An arrogant spirit will smother any expression of love, but a humble heart overflows with acts of love without even trying. What makes a person humble? Some seem to have it, and others don't. Should I just pray for it and hope I wake up some morning a more humble man? I don't think so. Humility, like all attributes of love, can be nurtured. Here's my top ten list of tips on how to "grow low," how to stimulate a spirit of humility.

1. *Study the nature of God.* It will convince you that a god you are not! We all need to remember in whose image we were created and how far we have fallen. *Start with the classic* Knowing God *by J. I. Packer.*

2. *Study the nature of man.* It is humbling to see who we are apart from the grace of God. *Start with Romans, chapters 1–3.*

3. *Study sin and grace.* A deeper understanding of grace humbles us by reminding us that salvation is a gift, undeserved and unearned. *Start with Ephesians 2:1–10 or Romans 3:21–5:21.*

4. *Study the fruit of the Spirit.* Examining our character against this great list will convince us that there is indeed work to be done. *Start with Galatians 5:13–26.*

5. *Study the profile of a disciple.* A study of the disciplines of the Christian life humbles anyone who will take an honest look at himself. *Start with John 15 and memorize verse 5.*

6. *Study the Ten Commandments.* This summation of God's moral law still stands as a tablet of truth that shows me my sin and reminds me that I cannot go it alone. *You'll find it in Exodus 20.*

7. *Study the Sermon on the Mount.* As Jesus sought to humble the religious leaders of His day with this great message, see if it doesn't have the same effect on you. *Read Matthew 5–7 and listen to the spirit of the law.*

8. *Study the kenosis of Christ.* Be humbled by the supreme illustration of true humility: the incarnation, suffering, and sacrifice of Christ. *Use Philippians 2:3–8.*

9. *Study the struggle with the flesh.* As Paul de-

scribes his own struggle with the flesh, be humbled that you can identify with his battle more than you'd care to admit. *The classic passage is Romans 7:14–25.*

10. *Study spiritual warfare.* The reality that our battle is not against flesh and blood drives us to a humble spirit of dependence, not arrogance. *Ephesians 6:10–20 is the place to go.*

Love is humble. Any investment you make in nurturing humility will pay big dividends throughout your life as you seek to love others.

Second, love free of arrogance inflates others instead of itself. Love that is not arrogant shifts its focus onto others. If arrogance has a reputation for being the center of attention, then love enjoys putting other people in the limelight. It pumps up the other guy. In biblical jargon, love edifies. Earlier in Paul's letter to the church of Corinth he issues this warning:

> Knowledge makes arrogant, but love edifies. (1 Corinthians 8:1)

The contrast he makes is between knowledge and love, arrogance and edification. The apostle is certainly not against knowledge in and of itself. But knowledge becomes dangerous if it partners with a prideful, arrogant attitude. Paul has already told us that even absolute, unrestricted knowledge is worthless without love (1 Corinthians 13:2). But love has great value, because in humility it seeks to lift up, encourage, or inflate others. It pumps them back up when they are deflated by life's sharp edges. In the process, their hope is restored.

Sometimes being an encourager isn't easy. Hope is hard to find. At times like these, I'd offer two suggestions for getting the words of encouragement and edification flowing.

1. *Focus on the positives you see in others.* Philippians 4:8 tells me what to look for in tough situations. No matter what the circumstance, this text has never failed to provide good guidance for edifying and encouraging others.

> *Finally, brethren, whatever is true, whatever is honorable, whatever is right, whatever is pure, whatever is lovely, whatever is of good repute, if there is any excellence and if anything worthy of praise, dwell on these things.*

If my mind is focused not on the negative but on this list of whatever is "worthy of praise," then my words will be messages of encouragement. Try it and test me in this. Select that slice of your life which is often a source of disappointment or discouragement, maybe even despair. Then get alone with God and ask Him to show you whatever is true, honorable, right, pure, lovely, of good repute, excellent, or worthy of praise. Now make a list. Write at least ten positives about the person or circumstance. Here's the trick. Let your mind dwell on those things. Meditate on them. In marital counseling, I require couples to post these top ten lists in a prominent place, read them over and over, and thank God for them at least three times a day.

A second tip for great encouragers . . .

2. *Focus on the untapped potential in people.* Loving encouragers always see more than is before their eyes. While the arrogant focuses on the unacceptable shortcomings of another, love edifies by spotlighting the underdeveloped potential. Love looks into the future and encourages others to see what it sees. Love sees people not as they are but as they can be.

In 1972 I attended a large gathering in Dallas, Texas, called Explo '72. I'll never forget the large leather belt one conferee was wearing. Engraved into the belt were the letters P.B.P.W.M.G.I.F.W.M.Y. That grabbed my curiosity, so I asked the stranger what the letters meant. He explained that he wore the belt to remind himself and others to "Please be patient with me. God isn't finished with me yet." Love would wear a belt like that. In fact, love would give them away as presents.

A story I've heard on several occasions illustrates the transforming power of words and actions that inflate or esteem another. It's the story of a guy named Johnny Lingo. Johnny, a most handsome fellow, lived in a day when men paid dowries to the fathers of the women they wished to wed. In one particular town, there lived a father who had three daughters, two of whom were sweet and lovely, and who each promised to fetch a handsome dowry. The third daughter, however, his eldest, was a different story. A typical dowry was a cow, and a one-cow woman was quite a woman indeed. But this father's sights were set much lower for his firstborn. If she could bring him a dozen eggs, or maybe a quart of milk, he'd be thrilled.

One day a stranger came to town. Johnny Lingo was his name. No sooner had Johnny set eyes on this plain young woman than he went straight to her father to seek her hand. "Will you accept twenty cows from me for the honor of marrying her?" Johnny asked. Stunned, the father quickly accepted, and not many days later the couple was married.

Word quickly spread around town of this enormous dowry. Suspecting that the stranger knew something they didn't, people began to look at the eldest daughter differently, as if there might be something special about her that they had missed all these years. She became the talk of the town's grapevine. Johnny Lingo, meanwhile, simply loved her, treating her in such a way that she knew he valued her highly. Of course, people continued to talk of the two in hushed conversations. Soon, however, the nature of their discussions began to change, because over time Johnny's bride began to change. As he continued to love and speak well of her, her view of herself slowly changed, and along with it, so did her behavior. She blossomed into a lovely lady . . . the twenty-cow woman Johnny had seen from the start.

Third, love free of arrogance admits its faults. Another characteristic of love, because it lacks arrogance, is that it *takes humility to a deeper level.* Loving this way means being willing to admit faults. Because it is not arrogant, love often and willingly says things like "I'm sorry" and "I guess I blew it." Like a recent Sunday morning at our house.

In this pastor's home, there's a pretty regular routine to Sunday mornings. Becky's an early riser, and since she gets up first, she usually puts on a pot of coffee. By the time I roll out of bed to review my notes and put any finishing touches on the day's sermon, that all-important first cup of coffee is just waiting to be poured. On this fateful Sunday, however, my internal alarm went off early, so I was uncharacteristically up and downstairs working at my desk while Becky snoozed contentedly. At this point the coffee was still in the can because, after all, I had this important sermon to preach to all these people, so I had gone straight to my desk when I got up, expecting Becky to be awake before too long.

Well, time passes and she isn't up, so I'm starting to get irritated. I'm thinking, *Hey, I need that cup of coffee now. I mean, I'm busy here with this message. Doesn't*

Beck realize that people are counting on me to serve them a healthy portion of spiritual food? She ought to . . . Just about then I look at my sermon title: "Love Has a Servant Spirit," and it hits me hard. Here I am so busy getting ready to tell our congregation how to be servant lovers that I miss my chance to actually be one myself. (In my meager defense, I can report that the next Sunday I intentionally got up first, brewed up the best pot of coffee for miles around, and delivered a cup to Becky in bed. Of course, after giving me a thank-you kiss, she cracked a little smile and asked, "Are you looking for a sermon illustration?")

A servant lover's first thought the first week would have been to make the coffee first. That's the beauty of a marriage where the couple functions in a nonarrogant way. It becomes a friendly battle to see who's going to serve whom. How sweet our marriage becomes when Becky knows beyond question that I regularly, joyfully choose to give up my agenda to serve her. "You just don't let me serve you enough" should be love's continual complaint.

In a world where getting an edge up on the next guy often draws more praise than lending him a helping hand, this kind of servant mentality can inject new life, not only into relationships, but into entire organizations. Not only do servant-minded people have no time for arrogance—they have no need for it either.

chapter five

Love Does Not Act Unbecomingly

LOVE IS NOT RUDE

If your home is like ours, there are certain sounds, behaviors, and bodily functions every member of the family learned at an early age were inappropriate in public settings. If your home includes junior high–age kids, especially boys, you also know that these sounds and behaviors are more popular with young adolescents than we parents wish they were. I'll spare you the specifics and trust your experience to make the point—that these taboos are some of the best present-day examples of a very broad category that Paul labels unbecoming behavior.

It's in the spirit of restating a point to make it abundantly clear that Paul takes us from the specific ("Love does not brag and is not arrogant") to the more general ("love does not act unbecomingly"). The braggadocio and haughtiness covered in the previous chapter are two good examples of undesirable behavior, but there are plenty more.

The Greek word we read as "unbecoming" is *aschemoneo;* the King James Version translates it as "unseemly," or in poor taste. The Greek root literally means "without shape" but is always used in the New Testament to refer to behavior that is "out of shape" or "out of bounds." By contrast, the opposite form of this term is often translated "prominent" or "prominence." It's used to describe Joseph of Arimathea as a "prominent member of the council," able to request the body of Christ from Pilate in Mark 15:43. Acts 17:12 uses the same term in reference to men and women of "prominence" who became believers. These were honorable or noble men and women of the city, leaders who had the respect of their friends and neighbors. They were the movers and shakers in the best sense of the term. People whose good taste, class, style, and reputation caused others to sit up and listen when they spoke.

By contrast, the unseemly often lack that style and grace which earns a great reputation. They say the wrong things at the wrong times in the wrong places. We all know the type. Webster's says that unbecoming means "unsuitable" or "improper," which prompts a definition that puts it in terms anyone can understand:

does not act unbecomingly · love that has good manners

This is where the rubber meets the road in relationships. It's a matter of manners. "Morals shown in conduct" is how the dictionary defines manners. I like the way the *New International Version* puts it: "Love . . . is not rude."

Now don't pass this off as old-fashioned, outdated advice. All of us do the good manners routine when we're dating, right? Love, guys, opens the door for a lady. Love, ladies, buys special gifts for that special guy.

How much, though, do we change our behavior toward our beloved after we marry? It's a scary thought, isn't it?

Love has good manners, and we need to get back in the habit of practicing them with those we love. It's sure easy for me to get out of these habits. There was a time when I told Becky I'd never stop opening doors for her. Then we got to that phase of family life when we both had a kid to carry. We were in the same boat, so manners didn't seem to matter so much. Now the kids open their own doors, but sadly, so does Becky. Too often.

I'm convinced we need to teach our young men especially to honor women in a way that our society so seldom does—by practicing good manners with them. This has nothing to do with the issue of equality of women; it's a reflection of the high value we place on women. I like the way Emily Post said it: "Manners are a sensitive awareness of the feelings of others. If you have that awareness, you have good manners, no matter what fork you use."

WORDS THAT SAY, "I LOVE YOU"

Good manners should really be in every person's job description. They are expressed in countless ways, but five basic ones come to mind, all of which communicate the same message—I love you! Here are the expressions in no particular order.

"Please." "Gimme, gimme" is not in the servant lover's vocabulary. By contrast, "please" turns up repeatedly, and it speaks volumes. It says I'm not assuming, expecting, or demanding anything. I'm requesting, which means you can decide how you'll respond. Saying "please" is a signal that you're granting your loved one freedom from control, freedom to choose. You're also communicating the servant attitude of authentic love. Notice how this

attitude is expressed in the prescribed leadership style for church leaders.

> Shepherd the flock of God among you, exercising oversight not under compulsion, but voluntarily, according to the will of God; ... nor yet as lording it over those allotted to your charge, but proving to be examples to the flock. (1 Peter 5:2–3)

Imagine the impact on a relationship if this type of attitude is allowed to trickle down from one to the other. If those in leadership, those with God-given authority, are to avoid exercising a bossy, "I'm in charge; do it 'cause I say so" attitude, surely this applies to the rest of us as well. Saying "please" may just be the simplest way to honor another person. I try to keep this in mind whenever I ask someone to do something, whether it's asking our son Paul to haul the trash cans to the street or asking my secretary to prepare a letter for my signature. Whether the request is going on a handwritten note or voice mail, I've found that the best word to begin with is "please."

"Thank you." What's the quickest way to say you value someone? Using this phrase gets my vote. It says you appreciate what's been done, what's been given. Sometimes we fail to say thanks because what we've received is so ordinary or everyday or expected. Say it anyway, because too often we overlook the best gifts people give us, whether they be things we can hold in our hands or less tangible gifts like time, kindness, or patience. I once wrote a brief letter of commendation to the supervisor of a computer company service technician who had been especially patient and efficient in helping me troubleshoot a complex hardware problem over the phone. The technician actually sent me a thank-you note, saying she was the talk of the office because people just never do

things like that. It even opened a door for me to share why I took the time to show my appreciation with a note of thanks. Here is the letter I E-mailed back to her.

Mindy,

    Thanks for taking the time to "thank me" for the "thank you" letter. I guess this is a short "thanks for the thank me for the thank you." Don't worry, I'm just kidding and not really a nut. I do want to explain the reason I was so patient.

    As the father of a high school daughter (Beth, a senior), I can tell you that my patience is not always that strong. But my attitudes have been shaped by a personal relationship with Jesus Christ as my Savior that began to change my life as a high school student in 1971. So I want to give Christ the credit lest you think I am just naturally patient.

    If you wish to know more about my faith, I suggest you check out the web page of the church I currently pastor in Fullerton, California, the First Evangelical Free Church of Fullerton. It's a wonderful church of 4,000 members, previously pastored by a man named Chuck Swindoll, a well-known Christian author and speaker. I am thankful for my family and current ministry, and I'm glad I could help you.

    Check out the web page at www.fefcful.org. Please let me know what you think. The web page has my picture and the E-mail addresses of our 16 other pastors, including our high school pastor, Eric Heard. If any of us can help you understand how to have a personal relationship with Christ or find a good church in your area, feel free to E-mail any of us.

    Thanks for serving my family,

                        H. Dale Burke, Pastor

Expressing thanks is equally appropriate for the more significant, even overwhelming acts of love that you've received from another. Consider Paul's words to some of the early churches.

In everything give thanks; for this is God's will for you in Christ Jesus. (1 Thessalonians 5:18)

Be filled with the Spirit, speaking to one another in psalms and hymns and spiritual songs, singing and making melody with your heart to the Lord; always giving thanks for all things in the name of our Lord Jesus Christ to God, even the Father. (Ephesians 5:18b–20)

The message is clear. Giving thanks is woven throughout the language of love. It should show up when we speak with one another . . . and when we speak with the God of love.

But thanks be to God, who always leads us in triumph in Christ, and manifests through us the sweet aroma of the knowledge of Him in every place. (2 Corinthians 2:14)

Be thankful to God and one another. Why? Because it's downright rude to receive and not say "thanks." Love says "please" and "thank you." Here's a third key word for loving with good manners.

"Excuse me" or *"I'm sorry."* I have no *right* to interrupt, bully my way through a crowd, or "bump" into a conversation. If I decide it's necessary to break into your space or your conversation, I need to remind myself that you have the floor and that a mild apology is appropriate. I love a line one of our friends uses when people forget their manners: "I've got one nerve, and you're on it!"

Have you ever been walking in a crowd and had someone slam into you, then just keep on walking as if nothing had happened? I have, and I'll have to admit that my first thought about the offender wasn't a pleasant one. I was fuming, and I was tempted to track him down and demand an apology. No, I didn't actually go after the guy, but I was hot. Now, just think how quickly my fuse would have fizzled if that bump had been followed by a quick, "Excuse me." Issue resolved . . . immediately! I'd walk away thinking, "What a nice guy . . . clumsy, but polite!"

If such a casual encounter with a stranger can so quickly surface heated emotions, it doesn't take a clinical psychologist to see the danger of failing to practice this common courtesy with people with whom we have an intimate relationship. In the former case, the experience may cause an inconvenience; but in the latter, it can be downright hurtful.

Let's say, for example, that I'm out shopping with my wife Becky, but as we're walking along, my thoughts are on a sticky point in the sermon I'm preparing for Sunday. Just as I'm trying to recall the definition of a Greek word, out of the corner of my eye I spot the store we were headed for, and I reflexively make a right-hand turn for the door, brushing right past Becky as I begin to let myself in. It's at this point that I come to my senses and notice Becky looking a little incredulous at my insensitivity. At this point I also hope my next reflex response would be to say, "Excuse me," and hold the door for my wife. If I simply plow ahead, rationalizing that I'm halfway through the door anyway, well, it would probably be better, to borrow a word picture from Jesus, if a giant doorknob were tied around my neck and I were thrown into the sea!

Seriously, how we respond after committing minor offenses can have major repercussions—positive and negative—in our love relationships. The right response actually does double duty. It acknowledges an offense, reflecting humility on our part, then corrects the offense, granting honor to the other person. While the offenses implied in 1 John 1:9 are far more serious than the ones we're discussing here, the spirit of the response is the same.

*If we confess our sins, He is faithful and righteous to forgive us our
sins and to cleanse us from all unrighteousness.*

When we blow it, miss the mark, fail to do or be what
God calls us to do or be, we've sinned. God says it's good
to confess it. The Greek term for "confession" means "to
agree with God" concerning our sin. The wisdom of
Scripture says don't delay. Come to God quickly and
honestly with a repentant spirit. When we do, 1 John 1:9
guarantees that the response of the Father is forgiveness
and restoration. A sincere "I'm sorry" accelerates the
healing process like the best of antibiotics, ointments, or
creams.

Without confession, the offense festers untreated
like an infection under the skin. Left untreated, it can
spread its poison throughout the body, eventually
threatening life itself.

*When I kept silent about my sin, my body wasted away
Through my groaning all day long.
For day and night Your hand was heavy upon me;
My vitality was drained away as with the fever heat of summer.*
                                        (Psalm 32:3–4)

But when I offer my God a sincere "I'm sorry," the
wound is cleansed by grace. Healing and restoration can
then commence. David affirms this in verse 5 of the
psalm: "I acknowledged my sin to You, and my iniquity I
did not hide; I said, 'I will confess my transgressions to
the Lord'; and You forgave the guilt of my sin."

My point is that it's not only good theology to say "I'm
sorry," it's good manners as well. If it's therapeutic for our
relationship, then let's generously apply the "Excuse me,
I'm sorry" ointment to all wounds great and small.

"Can I help you?" Especially these days, when too

many of us seem too preoccupied with ourselves, the use of this phrase carries with it the element of surprise that qualifies it as one of those random acts of kindness. And the accompanying kind action—whether it's opening a door, helping to push a stalled car out of a busy intersection, or doing the dinner dishes—conveys an important message loud and clear: "Someone cares!" Specifically, *you* care, and when that's the case, you tell people you love them by letting them know it.

You never know the impact your willing, helping hand may have in a relationship. I once heard of how the owner of several luxury hotels hired a young man to manage his newest one simply because the guy once went out of his way to serve the owner without realizing who he was. Reminds me of that verse in Hebrews.

> *Do not neglect to show hospitality to strangers, for by this some have entertained angels without knowing it. (13:2)*

What an inspiring thought—that in helping others you and I might actually have an opportunity to serve one of God's angels. Try something the next time you happen upon a stranger who is struggling with a box or who has just dropped a heavy load. The modern mind-set says, "Mind your own business, step around, and move on. After all, it's not your mess. In fact, look the other way as if you don't even notice." But love practices good manners, and good manners stop to help.

"You go first." No display of good manners is more loving, or more Christian, than this one. These are words that, when spoken sincerely, can only flow from a servant's heart. (Never mind the biblical principle that says that the last shall be first. That's intended to be a statement of fact, not a motivation for behavior.) Jesus did such a magnificent job of modeling this mandate.

Remember the feeding of the five thousand? His concern was that the multitude was fed before He or the disciples ate their meals. Meeting others' needs was a priority for Him, as it should be for us.

Once again, this runs counter to our culture. "Me first" is the predominant attitude. It's also one of the easiest sentences for a toddler to utter, as illustrated in the following list I received from a friend.

TODDLER PROPERTY LAWS

1. If I like it, it's mine.
2. If it's in my hand, it's mine.
3. If I can take it from you, it's mine.
4. If I had it a little while ago, it's mine.
5. If it's mine, it must never appear to be yours in any way.
6. If I'm doing something or building something, all the pieces are mine.
7. If it looks just like mine, it's mine.
8. If I think it's mine, it's mine.

We scan grocery checkout lines in search of the one that will let us be as close to the front as possible. People will line up and camp out days or even weeks to be first in line for tickets to certain events. Whatever the venue, our natural selfishness can be all too easily coaxed out of hiding. Choosing to let another go first, on the other hand, is a matter of choice. It's an act of the will.

Many of us were reminded of this reality as we watched the hit movie *Titanic*. When that ship was sinking, the majority of passengers headed for what turned out to be too few lifeboats. At that point, I was certainly struck by the love displayed by those who stepped aside to let others go first. Most dramatic in their unselfishness were the musicians who not only refused to jockey for position in the queue to safety but kept playing to calm the panicked crowd. What honorable men they were.

How might we imitate their example? Again, it could be simple common courtesies like allowing a loved one to be served first or giving a sibling first choice from the plate of turkey at Thanksgiving. It could also be letting another speak first as you're trying to work out a problem in your friendship. However and wherever you do it, stepping aside for another will always prove to be a great investment in your relationship with that person.

There you have it—a rundown of good manners. Each one illustrates love that does not act unbecomingly. Why does love behave this way? Because it is deeply concerned with the feelings of others, and the best way to let people know you love them is to *show* them you love them. Unlike Cuba Gooding Jr.'s memorable line from the movie *Jerry Maguire,* "Show me the money," people today need us to show them the love—God's love. And good manners is a great way to do it.

chapter six

Love Does Not Seek Its Own

A SERVANT SPIRIT

Love gets people's attention for one simple reason: It's different; it sticks out in the crowd. When the crowd is pushy, love is patient. When the crowd is cruel, love is kind. If the crowd is jealous, love is gently trusting. The crowd's envy highlights love's eagerness to trust that God knows what's best. An arrogant crowd clamors for attention while love is looking to shine the spotlight on someone else. The crowd forgets that manners matter, only to find love opening the door and leading the way with a "please" or "thank you." And the contrast continues.

When Paul writes that love "does not seek its own," he lifts love yet another notch higher. And while he doesn't belabor the point, his choice of words underscores it. A more literal rendering might be "Love does not seek to further its own profit or advantage." Blunt English translation: Love is not selfish. And those who are not selfish stick out in any crowd these days. Like when you step up to a grocery line with just two items and the lady

ahead of you with fifteen invites you to go ahead of her.
Or when the guy on a bus stands up to offer his seat to a
young mother holding her infant in one arm and a shopping bag in the other.

At one extreme end of unselfishness is heroism,
which is so rare that some cities give awards to the people who display it. Who could forget the ill-fated teams
who set out to scale Mount Everest in May 1996? Three
teams were climbing simultaneously. A member of one
team, Anatoli Boukreev, had been hired by Everest
climbing veteran Scott Fischer to help with his expedi-
tion. Shortly before a late afternoon blizzard swept in
that ultimately killed eleven of the climbers, Boukreev
descended to the group's highest camp to get more oxygen tanks for those who had reached the summit and
were on their way back down. When the storm struck,
he headed up again but had to return to the camp and
wait for the weather to clear. At an altitude well in ex-
cess of five miles, with seventy-mile-an-hour winds and
temperatures plummeting to –40 degrees, he saw no
other options. But when his friend and climbing partner
Neal Biedelman stumbled into camp at one in the morning, Boukreev could wait no longer. He set out in search
of other survivors and spent the rest of the night rescu-
ing those he found, carrying some of the unconscious
ones on his back, leading others, exhausted but still able
to walk, down the trail to safety. At five in the morning,
with his entire team (except Fischer) safe, Boukreev
collapsed, exhausted.

JESUS—THE ULTIMATE SERVANT

Spanning the spectrum of unselfishness from small
selfless acts to heroic feats like Boukreev's, we find our
model for this type of loving behavior. Listen as Paul

presents this model in his letter to another New Testament church.

> Do nothing from selfishness or empty conceit, but with humility of mind regard one another as more important than yourselves; do not merely look out for your own personal interests, but also for the interests of others. Have this attitude in yourselves which was also in Christ Jesus, who, although He existed in the form of God, did not regard equality with God a thing to be grasped, but emptied Himself, taking the form of a bond-servant, and being made in the likeness of men. Being found in appearance as a man, He humbled Himself by becoming obedient to the point of death, even death on a cross. (Philippians 2:3–8)

From "not merely looking out for your own personal interests" to "becoming obedient to the point of death," Jesus led the way for those who "do not seek their own." When writing to the church at Philippi, the term Paul uses to describe one who lives this way is, you guessed it, *servant,* and it provides an ideal definition for this next attribute of authentic love.

does not seek its own · love that has a servant spirit

Note that this is not a passive process, but an active one. It's not just sitting back and letting others go first; it's lifting others up, escorting them to the front of the line.

Once again, an attitude check is a prerequisite for developing this kind of behavior. If my attitude is "empty conceit," then I'm stuck on myself. I could care less about others. But if my attitude is humility, then it comes naturally to regard others as equally important, even more important than myself. A simple equation: Empty conceit leads to selfishness—humility leads to selflessness. So it follows that as I develop a humble spirit, I begin to look out for others.

MOTHER TERESA

We saw this sort of transformed life on brilliant display in Agnes Gonxha Bojaxhiu, a tiny Albanian nun whose selfless life of service to Calcutta's castoffs caused her to stand out in a crowd of millions. After founding The Missionaries of Charity there in 1950, she became Mother Teresa, and while she is gone now, her life's work stands as a living illustration of "love does not seek its own." What is so remarkable to Western observers like me is that this faith-filled Christian soldier learned this lesson of love before she was out of her teens. She explains how in an interview with Malcolm Muggeridge, published in 1971 in the book *Something Beautiful for God*.[1]

MUGGERIDGE: Mother Teresa, when did all this begin with you? I don't mean just your house here [referring to Kelighat, The House of the Dying where they take in and care for Calcutta's destitute]. But when did the feeling that you must dedicate yourself to poor people come to you?

MOTHER TERESA: It was many years ago when I was at home with my people.

MUGGERIDGE: When was that?

MOTHER TERESA: In Skopje in Yugoslavia. I was only twelve years old then. I lived at home with my parents; we children used to go to a non-Catholic school but we also had very good priests who were helping the boys and girls to follow their vocation according to the call of God.

It was then that I first knew I had a vocation to the poor.

MUGGERIDGE: That was when it all started.

MOTHER TERESA: Yes, in 1922.

MUGGERIDGE: It was then that you decided your life
was not to be one of pleasing yourself,
but was to be given to God in a very
special way.

MOTHER TERESA: I wanted to be a missionary. I wanted
to go out and give the life of Christ to
people in the missionary countries.

Notice Muggeridge's choice of words in describing
what he sees in this woman: "It was then that you decided your life was not to be one of pleasing yourself."
Sounds like a paraphrase of Philippians 2:4, doesn't it?
In another interview twenty-five years later, Mother
Teresa expressed her call in similarly compelling terms.
"The turning point came on September 10, 1946, when
[then] Sister Teresa was traveling by train to Darjeeling
to recuperate from tuberculosis. 'The message was quite
clear,' she said. 'I was to give up all and follow Jesus into
the slums. . . . It was an order. . . . And when that happens, the only thing to do is say yes.'"[2]

Like Mother Teresa, living in a way that says we do
not seek our own begins by thinking that way first. Do
we think of ourselves first (empty conceit), or do we
think of others first? The former amounts to selfishness;
the latter reflects humility. Again, it's a matter of attitude leading to action, of character shaping conduct.
Like the Bob Dylan song says, "Everybody gotta serve
somebody."[3] The question is, will we serve ourselves or
others? Paul says that love is more interested in serving
the other guy.

PRINCIPLES FROM THE EXAMPLE OF JESUS

If we look closely at Paul's challenge to the Philippians (2:5–11), we see Jesus displaying different aspects of a servant spirit. There are at least seven truths about serving in Philippians 2. Let's start with verse 5 and examine them.

Have this attitude in yourselves which was also in Christ Jesus. (v. 5)

1. As we've just said, *servanthood is an attitude, not just an act.* Servant love is tough to fake. If you want to act like a servant, first you have to think like one. You must adopt a radical new attitude toward yourself, others, and God Himself. Jesus "considered others more important than himself." That's attitude. It's an attitude of esteeming or elevating not myself but others. It's an attitude of caring, not just about my needs, but about the needs of others. This attitude keeps on the watch, always alert, "not merely look[ing] out for your own personal interests, but also for the interests of others" (v. 4). The *acts* of the servant are only needed *occasionally,* but the *attitude* of a servant *must always be active.* Without the attitude, the best opportunities to love by serving will most likely go unnoticed.

Who, although He existed in the form of God, did not regard equality with God a thing to be grasped. (v. 6)

2. What's he saying here? That *being a servant is not about weakness; it's about strength.* One who "existed in the form of God" is hardly operating from a position of weakness. There's a misconception these days that if I become the servant of another person, then I'm the

weak one in the relationship. But in Jesus, the opposite is true. As God, He chose to take the role of a servant. There is power in that kind of choice. The best servants serve out of their strengths. In fact, the value of servants is precisely that they have competence and abilities—strengths—that can be used to serve their masters.

Equality with God [is not] a thing to be grasped. (v. 6)

3. Here he's underscoring the idea that *servanthood is not about insecurity, but security*. A Christlike servant has to be secure to exhibit excellence in his behavior toward others. Such servants are so secure that they are willing to do whatever their master asks, because they have no one to impress except the one they have chosen to serve. It's as if Jesus were saying, "They don't really get the picture about why I'm here. They don't really realize who I am. But that doesn't matter. I don't need their applause to feel secure in My role here. I'm happy to give up the perks that come with deity so that I can serve these people whom I love." Why? Because in serving us, He was serving His Father in heaven. So it is when we serve others.

He ... emptied Himself, taking the form of a bondservant, and being made in the likeness of men. (v. 7)

4. Too often people view servants as victims. Jesus has a different take on this. He tells us that *servanthood is not about being taken advantage of, and its not about being "taken"; it's about being "given."* Real servants, like Jesus, willingly give up their rights, their privileges, their time, and their agendas to meet the needs of others.

Being found in appearance as a man, He humbled Himself. (v. 8a)

5. *Servanthood is not about taking care of my world; it's about entering the world of those I seek to serve,* just like Mother Teresa did. Maybe the world you're being asked to enter is uncomfortable. Unpleasant. Inhospitable. How instructive is Mother Teresa's perspective. Muggeridge mentioned to her that it seemed "extraordinary that one person could just walk out and decide to tackle" something like the pain and poverty of Calcutta. She replied, "I was so sure then, and I'm still convinced, that it is he and not I. That's why I was not afraid; I knew that if the work was mine it would die with me. But I knew that it was his work, that it will live and bring much good."[4]

He … humbled himself by becoming obedient to the point of death, even death on a cross. (v. 8a)

6. But Jesus did more than become a man; He became "obedient to the point of death." *Being a servant is not about being a doormat; it's about becoming a sacrifice.* There's a big difference between the two. You see, doormats aren't very exciting. They just lie there and wait to be stepped on. A sacrifice, though, is dramatically different. A willing sacrifice is active, alive. It's on the move, always choosing to go where it's needed most. Which means that unlike the demeaning boredom of a doormat lifestyle, sacrificial living can be downright exciting. It accomplishes something significant, which is to make ministry happen. It moves God's kingdom forward. Granted, in the process you might get stepped on, but in doing so you just might become a stepping-stone to advance someone closer to Christ.

Therefore also God highly exalted Him ... to the glory of God the Father. (vv. 9, 11)

7. This is the core of Paul's message in these verses. Ultimately, we serve for one, and only one, reason. To glorify God. *Being a servant is not about pleasing the person I'm serving; it's about pleasing God.* When Jesus gave His body and shed His blood, He displayed not only infinite love for us but an intense desire to please His Father in heaven. True, He met our needs on the cross, but His motivation was obedience, not to us, but to God. Jesus was driven to please the One who sent Him.

There's a great parallel here for you and me, because often when we try to serve, the question becomes one of motivation. If I'm doing it only to please the person I'm serving, chances are I'm looking for some kind of payback. Oh, nothing big, of course. A word of appreciation will do. A gift certificate? That would be fine, sure, but hey, whatever. However subtle the expectation, if I give expecting a return and it never comes, what happens? That's right—I stop giving. I become resentful. That's what makes Jesus' model so superior. If my motive in giving, if my desire in serving, is to please and glorify God, then regardless of the response from those being served, I experience God's pleasure, which prompts me to serve again. And again.

Let's review the contrasting characteristics we've discussed that distinguish servant lovers. There are seven of them. Servant love . . .

is an **attitude,** not just an **act**
operates from **strength,** not from **weakness**
is **secure,** not **insecure**
is about **being "given,"** not about **being taken**

is about **entering your world,** not about **taking care
of my world**
is about being a **sacrifice,** not about being a **doormat**
is about **pleasing God,** not about **pleasing people**

This is love that has a servant spirit. How ironic that
what sounds like a prescription for unfulfillment is actually your ticket to powerful living. Pick your extreme sport
—skydiving off mountaintops, driving a jet-powered car
through the sound barrier, whatever. Those kinds of
thrills flicker and fade, but the fulfillment that comes
from serving the Maker of the universe is what life's all
about. Hymn writers Gloria and Bill Gaither said it well
when they wrote these words:

> I will serve Thee, because I love Thee,
> You have given life to me;
> I was nothing before You found me,
> You have given life to me.
> Heartaches, broken pieces,
> Ruined lives are why You died on Calvary;
> Your touch is what I longed for,
> You have given life to me.

"I Will Serve Thee." Words by William J. And Gloria Gaither. Music
by William J. Gaither. Copyright © 1969 Gaither Music Company. All
rights controlled by Gaither Copyright Management. Used by permission.

SUSAN

Being involved in pastoral ministry, I regularly have
the privilege of seeing this kind of servant-love on display. Sometimes, however, the degree to which people
are willing to love humbles you deeply, as was the case
of our friend Susan (not her real name). Susan came to
faith in Jesus Christ at our church. As she got connected,

we got to know her better and discovered that she was often alone. Her husband, Bill (not his name), a pharmacist and not a Christian, was a highly successful, hard-driving workaholic. His typical work week was six and a half long days. His limited time off was often spent doing projects or watching sports.

Despite the obvious deficiencies in her marriage, Susan the young Christian decided to love and serve Bill just as he was and to trust God to be the One who changed him. Years passed. Bill didn't change. Yet Susan remained firm in her conviction. "Why don't you just leave him?" friends would ask. But Susan had an unshakable resolve. "As I grew in my faith," she told me one day, "I realized that each one of us has a unique way to glorify God. Instead of doing it through a good marriage, maybe mine was to do it through a bad one."

One day a doctor whose prescriptions Bill had filled for many years passed away. A few days after his death, two tough looking guys showed up at one of Bill's pharmacies and made a shocking demand. "That doctor you supplied drugs to was supplying them to us," they said. "Now you're going to sell them to us." To convince him that they meant business, the thugs described Bill's daughter and assured him that they knew where he lived, saying that if he wanted his family to be safe, he'd cooperate with them. Unwisely, he did, until the day some detectives showed up at his store to question him. Turns out they'd been dogging those drug dealers for months and had finally traced them to Bill's pharmacy.

That day Bill had to come home and tell Susan the whole sorry story, including the very real possibility that he'd be going to prison. Again, she had to decide whether to leave him or love him. "If Jesus Christ was willing to love me as is and to save me, how could I not love you now?" she told him. At that point, Bill was absolutely overwhelmed at Susan's capacity to keep loving him, and he responded in the most logical way possible. He wanted Christ as his Savior too.

As he grew in his faith, his wife saw a new husband and father emerge. But as he grew, Bill's loving acts as a husband and father were to take place from a prison cell. When he got out, he had lost his pharmacy license and much of his wealth and property, but he had gained a transformed life. Today, he is rebuilding with a wife who still loves him and serving in a church where he, too, is growing as a servant lover.

And we are left to ask, What would have happened if Susan had walked out on her husband and her marriage? The answer is obvious. But now, by God's grace, she has what she hoped for . . . and love is the reason.

NOTES

1. Malcolm Muggeridge, *Something Beautiful for God* (New York: Harper & Row, 1971), 83–84.
2. Mother Teresa, interview by Daphne Barak, *Ladies Home Journal*, April 1966, 146.
3. Bob Dylan, "Gotta Serve Somebody," Copyright © 1979 Special Rider Music. All rights reserved.
4. Muggeridge, *Something Beautiful for God*, 88.

chapter seven

Love
Is Not
Provoked

LOVE HAS A SLOW FUSE

One of the best things about having a best friend is that if you're having a bad day or you're in a bad mood and you unwisely take it out on your best friend, you usually get away with it. "It is one of the blessings of old friends that you can afford to be stupid with them," Ralph Waldo Emerson observed, and he was right. It takes a lot to provoke a friend to anger. In this regard, friendship is very much like a fuse. The longer it is, the more time it takes for things to blow up. Of course this means that the opposite is also true. Short friendships, or the absence of friendship, is like a short fuse. Let's call this Burke's axiom.

My friend and coauthor, Jac, says his best friend in high school proved that this axiom is actually true. Jac's friend (we'll call him Bob to protect his family name) fit every reasonable criteria for being a best friend. In good times or bad, whether Jac was behaving well or behaving stupidly, Bob bore with him. It helped that Bob was

mild-mannered by nature. At least that's how he con-
ducted himself with his best friend Jac. But one day Bob
happened to run into another guy. Actually, the guy ran
into Bob, intentionally. This guy's clear desire was to
provoke him. Now Jac had bumped into Bob dozens of
times. Even knocked him to the floor once or twice.
Usually Bob just laughed. His fuse fizzled. But when
this other guy did the bumping, he got a different reaction. At first, Bob said coolly but politely, "At least you
could say excuse me." The guy's unfortunate response
was to give Bob a little shove. Provocation number two.
At this point, Jac says, Bob "kind of went crazy." It took
three guys to pull him off his provoker.

When the apostle Paul wrote in verse 5 that love "is
not provoked," he meant that whether it's with a friend
or an enemy, you shouldn't react the way Bob did. Paul
was identifying an emotion that has the potential to do
quick and serious damage if allowed to flare up and out
of control.

The Greek word translated "provoke" is *paroxuno*, a
combination of *para* (beside or along side of) and oxus
(sharp as in a sword or sickle). You allow yourself to be
provoked when the words or actions of another pene-
trate your spirit, pricking or stabbing you as a sharpened
sword wounds an enemy. To use a common metaphor,
you let it get under your skin. Love refuses to allow the
sharp words or hurtful acts of another to find their way
into the heart, do their damage, and leave their scars.

To be provoked, on the other hand, means to let another person's words or actions rouse or incite you to
anger. Serious anger. Violent and vindictive anger. Sa-
vory anger that you're unwilling to release. By caution-
ing us against it, Paul is saying that *unchecked anger can
be hazardous to the health of your most cherished rela-*

tionships. So a definition of what he's driving at might look like this:

is not provoked · love that has a slow fuse

In layman's terms, "love has a slow fuse," and at no time is a slow fuse more of an asset than when we get upset. Anger is one of our trickier emotions. Sometimes when feeling angry we try to convince ourselves that it's no big deal—that Christians shouldn't let silly things bother them. Just ignore it and it'll go away. Don't believe it. With human beings, anger is part of every relationship and must be processed. And it's not just between enemies that anger lurks in the shadows. Wherever there are friendships, marriages, and families, anger is waiting to pounce, because any relationship brings with it the potential to be let down, disappointed, mistreated, or worse. Anger is a menace that continually threatens. To deny that threat is like swimming among sharks with an open wound on your foot. Eventually, you will feel the bite! Listen to Paul's words:

> Be angry, and yet do not sin; do not let the sun go down on your anger, and do not give the devil an opportunity. (Ephesians 4:26–27)

OK, you say, anger is inevitable. You don't deny it. So does that mean we're doomed to perpetual friction and turmoil in our relationships? Not at all. The same apostle who says "Love has a slow fuse" is the one who wrote to the Ephesian church, "Be angry, and yet do not sin" (Ephesians 4:26). How can I avoid sin when I'm feeling angry? In other words, how can I lengthen my fuse so it doesn't blow when I'm feeling ticked? If we keep a short fuse, verse 27 warns us we're going to get hammered! We've given the devil the "opportunity" to destroy our

relationships. The answer is: Deal with it! Don't ac-
knowledge it and then ignore it. Get it out in the open
and deal with it.

Your incentive for learning how to deal with anger is
likely to increase as you gain a clearer view of the damage it can cause. It's like when you buy homeowner's insurance. The sales rep usually starts by making it crystal
clear what you're going to have to pay if your house
burns down. Once you see that the fire can wipe you
out, you're motivated to do whatever it takes to protect
yourself. With anger, the potential damage is calculated
in terms of injured emotions, broken friendships, and
fractured families. Let the anger escalate like a fuse out
of control, and the risk runs more toward the physical,
with murder being the worst-case scenario. Is anger
worth learning to control? When you dare to count the
cost, the answer becomes frighteningly obvious. Like
putting out a fire, the key is to spot it when it's small and
knock it down quickly.

WHEN ANGER BECOMES SIN

Getting back to Paul's comment to the Ephesians,
when does anger become sin? Isn't all anger sin? Isn't it
unchristian or ungodly to get angry? I don't think so, unless you want to accuse Jesus Christ of sinning or of being unchristian. He definitely felt the fire of anger when
He cleared the money changers out of the temple. God
Himself got extremely upset with those He loved. Exodus 4:14 says that "the anger of the Lord burned against
Moses." Angry feelings are not in and of themselves sin.
The emotion of anger is often a natural response to unjust or unrighteous treatment. But when those emotions
lead to unloving, vengeful actions or attitudes, we sin. If
we look at a short sentence in the letter Paul wrote to

the church at Colossae, I think the answer to the question of when anger is sin becomes apparent:

> But now you also, put them all aside: anger, wrath, malice, slander, and abusive speech from your mouth. (Colossians 3:8)

The feeling of anger becomes sin when we allow it to escalate, when we allow it to control us instead of taking the initiative to rein it in. If we don't take control, if once our anger is kindled we allow it to keep burning, then it shoots up flames of wrath, malice, slander, and abusive speech. These are all used in the biblical text to represent sin, the kind of behaviors that Paul says are things "in [which we] once walked" and to which we are to "consider the members of [our] earthly [bodies] as dead" (Colossians 3:7, 5).

CONTROLLING YOUR ANGER

Practice honesty. Controlling your anger takes work, sometimes very hard work. You need to be deliberate and diligent to keep this fiery emotion contained. And your first line of defense is honesty.

> Therefore, laying aside falsehood, speak truth each one of you with his neighbor, for we are members of one another. (Ephesians 4:25)

Expressing my feelings of anger to the one who hurt me is the first step to extinguishing anger before it gets out of control. Speaking the truth must take place at several levels. It requires, for instance, being honest about the little irritations that can undermine a relationship when left unaddressed. It requires a willingness to speak up and say so when comments are made that hurt someone in the relationship. And it demands that you lovingly confront behavior that is inappropriate or unhealthy for the relationship.

Another critical component of honesty which, while it seems self-evident, can be easily overlooked is the refusal to speak untruth. Maybe you're tempted to twist the facts here or bend the truth there to avoid the pain of a hard conversation. Don't do it. The danger of allowing a string of little white lies to pile up is that in the long run you'll erode the trust between you and the one you love.

Speaking the truth also means being honest enough with yourself that you can admit when the heat is building. You can spot the embers of anger, which increases your chances of cooling them down before they burst into flames. Once you've identified it, how do you keep anger from elevating your emotional thermometer?

Here are four basics for controlling those emotions before they take control of you.

- First, *do your best to keep short accounts*. This serves to minimize the pent-up emotions that lead to anger. Becky and I take seriously the advice to "not let the sun go down on your anger." Anger makes a lousy mattress; don't sleep on it.
- When an incident does occur that dredges up those emotions, *think before you speak*. If you dump the whole emotional load first, without thinking, you'll spend more time than you care to imagine cleaning up the mess. The proverb is true: "A harsh word stirs up anger" (15:1).
- On the other hand, if you *start by first describing how you feel*, preferably in a controlled tone of voice, you're likely to create a cooler atmosphere and experience the first half of that proverb: "A gentle answer turns away wrath."

• *Seek resolution quickly.* Another line of defense for
preventing an anger buildup is to act *quickly when
anger strikes.* Anger left to fester becomes a deep
emotional infection that only gets worse as time
passes. Paul knew what he was talking about when
he advised, "Do not let the sun go down on your
anger" (Ephesians 4:26*b*). Seldom is an outburst of
anger caused by a single incident. More often it's
one or more unresolved issues that have been allowed to smolder below the surface. The devil rel-
ishes unresolved conflict. It's like tinder to him,
waiting to be ignited by behavior that in almost
any other situation would be harmless.

I remember with considerable embarrassment just
such an incident. Our first child, Beth, was only weeks
old as Mother's Day 1980 rolled around. As that important holiday approached, I did what every good son
should do. I sent my mother a card and probably a small
gift, then called to wish her a happy Mother's Day, after
which I figured I'd done well by the mother in my life.
Of course I learned later on that Becky expected our
new daughter to do something for her on Mother's Day.
But Beth didn't know that, and besides, she couldn't
drive yet. So, if you can believe it, my wife, the new
mother, didn't get a card or flowers or anything on her
first Mother's Day. I still can't believe that Beth was so
insensitive. (Yes, my tongue is firmly in my cheek.)

As you might imagine, this irritated Becky. She later
told me that she said to herself, "Well, this is silly. I
shouldn't let something so trivial bother me." The truth
is, it wasn't trivial, and it did bother her, but she never
told me. And pretty soon it began to smolder inside her.
Before long, the temperature in our home began to

drop, even though it was summertime and we didn't have air-conditioning. I didn't know why, but it was evident to me that our relationship had begun to cool, something which I began to resent. But unfortunately, I didn't say anything to Becky. Instead of expressing my frustration, I started acting cooler toward her too, which of course only made matters worse. Before long our marriage was in a deep freeze, and neither of us had expressed a word of frustration!

It all came to a head a few months later as we were driving home to visit our families in West Virginia for our summer vacation. "You know, honey," I said as we drove along, "I don't like the way we're feeling. I mean, our marriage . . . there's something wrong. What is it?"

"I don't know," was all she said at first.

We talked some more, and I finally asked, "Is there anything bugging you? Have I done something to make you mad?"

"Well, it's really silly," she said, "but . . ." and then she told me what I had done.

When she finished, I felt terrible. "Will you forgive me, honey?" I asked. "I can't believe I was so insensitive to you as a new mom. But there's something else. I need to confess that I made it worse because I was resentful of the way you've been acting, but I never said anything to you about my feelings either."

"I'm sorry I didn't communicate my anger to you earlier," was Becky's response, and before we had driven too many more miles, the issue was resolved and we had a great trip and a wonderful vacation. Looking back, it seems ridiculous that something so small had escalated to the point that our young marriage was close to being in serious trouble. All because of unresolved anger.

A THREE-POINT CHECKUP

If you're serious about preventing anger from escalating into sin, ask yourself why and how you're handling your feelings of anger. Then follow up with any appropriate adjustments to both your attitude and your behavior. Based on Ephesians 4:29–32, I can recommend the following three-point checkup. Let's start by reviewing the text:

> Let no unwholesome word proceed from your mouth, but only such a word as is good for edification according to the need of the moment, so that it will give grace to those who hear. Do not grieve the Holy Spirit of God, by whom you were sealed for the day of redemption. Let all bitterness and wrath and anger and clamor and slander be put away from you, along with all malice. And be kind to one another, tender-hearted, forgiving each other, just as God in Christ also has forgiven you.

Check your motives. We've all seen the in-your-face T-shirts and bumper stickers that say, "I don't get mad, I get even!" It may be short, but a statement like that says a lot, and its main message is that malice is my motive. But verse 29 says to speak "only such a word as is good for edification," to build up, not bring down. If I'm interested in hurting rather than healing, in revenge rather than reconciliation, then my anger has made me malicious. My motive has degenerated to being destructive rather than constructive. I'm sinning.

Check your timing. Paul says we are to speak "according to the need of the moment." The moment you're really angry may not be the ideal time to talk about the issues that are causing you to lose your cool. It's definitely not the best time for the person you're angry with to present you with a solution to the problem. At that moment there is too much danger of turning a flame of frustration into a wildfire of the worst order. Timing can also be a matter of location. Before confronting someone, it's a good idea to ask yourself not only if now is the right time but if this is the right place. In public is always the wrong place to work through your anger with another person.

Check your manner. Besides "let[ting] no unwholesome word proceed from your mouth," it's wise to follow Solomon's counsel when working through anger.

> *A gentle word turns away wrath, but a harsh word stirs up anger.*
> *(Proverbs 15:1)*

How refreshing if we're able to take this radically different approach. If we use "gentle words" instead of goading, if we do as Paul says and seek to be "kind to one another, tender-hearted," we'll increase our success rate at controlling, defusing, and even eliminating anger.

At the core of these three checkpoints is a goal that flows, yet again, from the heart of a servant. When our blood starts to boil, nothing will turn down the heat faster than a conscious desire to build up the person we're angry at, to speak words that are "good for edification." As we saw in an earlier chapter, this is one way to apply Paul's charge that you "not merely look out for your own personal interests, but also for the interests of others" (Philippians 2:4).

There's the balance you're looking for. In circumstances where anger threatens, "love is not provoked" because it cares equally about you *and* the person you love. Remember: Love has a slow fuse.

chapter eight

Love Does Not Take into Account a Wrong Suffered

LOVE FORGIVES

I ran across a list not too long ago entitled "Things We Can Learn from Our Dog." It included some great advice, like "never pass up the opportunity to go for a joy ride," "when you're happy, dance around and wag your entire body," and "eat with gusto and enthusiasm." The last three, though, added up to a great formula for working through anger and not taking into account a wrong suffered. Here they are:

- When someone is having a bad day, be silent, stick close by, and nuzzle them gently.
- Avoid biting when a simple growl will do.
- Never hold a grudge.

Pretty good advice, isn't it?

As we saw in the previous chapter, it is easier to say "love is not provoked" than to do it, and we have yet to talk about one huge reason for this difficulty. It's so huge

that Paul mentions it specifically: Love "does not take
into account a wrong suffered." What's he saying? The
King James Version's rendition of this phrase is that love
"thinketh no evil." What Paul's suggesting is that you
give a person who appears to have wronged you the ben-
efit of the doubt, but it's really much more than that. Of
course, one word says it best. Let's try that word for our
definition:

does not take into account a wrong suffered ·
love that forgives

Remember the last line in the Ephesians text in the
last chapter? "Forgiving each other, just as God in Christ
also has forgiven you" (4:32). Often the last and most
challenging step in controlling your anger is dealing directly with the cause of it through the process of forgiveness. If we're going to fully appreciate the challenge
here, we need a good grasp of the Greek term that we
render *forgive.*

The word in the Greek, *logizomai,* is an accounting
term that means "to take inventory, count, reckon, or
number." The fact is, love would make a terrible ac-
countant. It's not because love misses the math or mis-
takenly enters data on the wrong page. Love chooses to
keep no record of wrongs done against it. It doesn't need
to keep track of every debt, since it's not in the business
of collecting on overdue accounts. It doesn't need to
keep score because it's not intent on "evening the score."
Love knows that the real winner isn't the one who gets
even, but the one who forgives even when it's not deserved. That's grace unlimited.

Reality is, most of us struggle with forgiveness. We
live to get even. Keeping short accounts, even no accounts of wrongs done against us, can be a daunting as-

signment. So let's examine some of the "whats, whys and hows" of forgiveness.

WHAT IS FORGIVENESS?

There are two major elements to forgiveness found in Ephesians 4:32.

Be kind to one another, tender-hearted, forgiving each other, just as God in Christ also has forgiven you.

The first element of forgiveness is mercy, which simply means *not giving* someone what they *do* deserve. Even if we feel that a person's behavior toward us deserves a certain response, we choose to respond differently. That's mercy. This doesn't mean a reciprocal response isn't warranted. Sometimes, if a person has truly wronged us or sinned against us, he deserves our wrath. His behavior toward us, if returned in kind, would bring back on him the punishment he deserves. Then justice would be done. But when we hold back our bitterness and wrath —our anger, slander, and malice—when we choose not to punish, we're giving mercy. God showed us mercy when we deserved to die for our sin, but He sent Jesus to pay that price for us instead.

The second element of forgiveness is grace, which simply means *giving* someone something he *doesn't* deserve. So while mercy is not giving someone what he does deserve, grace is giving someone something he doesn't deserve. It's a subtle, but important, difference. When someone has been mean to me, when he's been nasty or out of sorts, then he doesn't deserve for me to respond with kindness, does he? So when I do respond kindly, I'm giving him what he doesn't deserve: kindness. That sort of response goes way beyond mercy. It's grace.

Grace is active, choosing to give back something, such as kindness. Or forgiveness. God showed us the grace side of forgiveness by extending eternal life to us through Jesus' death at Calvary. We don't deserve that gift of life; He gives it to us by grace.

WHY SHOULD WE FORGIVE?

The distinction between mercy and grace may help us to understand forgiveness better, but it doesn't answer a basic, yet monumental, question: Why should we forgive? Why not live like the bumper sticker says: "I don't get mad; I just get even"? There are plenty of reasons for forgiving, and they're all found in Ephesians 4:32 and the first two verses of Ephesians 5.

> *Be kind to one another, tender-hearted, forgiving each other, just as God in Christ also has forgiven you. (Ephesians 4:32)*

> *Therefore be imitators of God, as beloved children; and walk in love, just as Christ also loved you and gave Himself up for us, an offering and a sacrifice to God as a fragrant aroma. (Ephesians 5:1–2)*

Do you believe there are eight reasons in these few verses for choosing to forgive? Here they are.

1. *I forgive to obey God's will for my life.* Ephesians 5:1–2 begins by challenging us to forgive one another as God has forgiven us. It's a command. And I don't know about you, but over the years I've found that when God says, "Do it," His command is reason enough to forgive. Even if emotionally I don't want to do it, or intellectually it doesn't make sense to do it, God *says work at forgiving.*

2. *I forgive to share what I have freely received.* In Ephesians 5:2, the phrase "just as Christ also loved you" gives us not only the method of forgiving, but also the motivation. If I've really tasted forgiveness, then I should

pass it on to others. What if tomorrow morning a guy knocks at your door and says, "You don't know me, but here's a hundred dollar bill. Love ya." And you say, "Love you too, bud," just to be polite. And he walks off. You're thinking, *That was really strange. Nice, but strange.* Next morning, there's another knock at the door and it's the same guy. "Hey, you don't know me," he says again, "but here's another hundred." Now you're thinking, *Hmmm, I could get to like this guy.* What if he did the same thing every day for five years? Wouldn't that be great?

Now, after five years, let's say you respond to the knock at your door and it's another guy, looking kind of down on his luck, pushing a cart, and he says to you, "Could you spare twenty bucks? I need to get some gas for my car, and I'd like to get a meal for my family." But you say, "You know, my bills are kind of high and I'm a little tight this month. Sorry, I really can't help you."

Wrong! You should give the guy the money, right? How dare you be so cheap after receiving one hundred dollars a day for years! Is the gift of forgiveness any different? Which day of your life does God not give you forgiveness if you know Jesus Christ? Then all of a sudden someone wrongs you, hurts you—as we often hurt God—and God says that just as you've received it from Him, forgive another.

3. *I forgive to imitate my Father's example.* The text says, "Therefore be imitators of God, as beloved children" (Ephesians 5:1). I need to be a chip off the old block. I need to be imitating God the Father because I'm one of His children, and this passage says that one of the greatest ways to imitate God to a watching world is by forgiving when it's undeserved. That is the most godlike thing I can do.

When I was a child I used to play a game called cha-

rades. You're probably familiar with it. To play cha-
rades, you draw a slip of paper out of a box or a hat.
There's a word or phrase on that paper, like the word
cow. Your challenge is to get the other people on your
team to say "cow," so you try to imitate a cow. But you
can't say anything. You can't even moo. As I recall, imitating a cow wasn't too tough, but what if the word you
drew out of the hat was *God?* What would you do?

Difficult or not, this passage we've just read says
we're to imitate God. How? By walking in love. And how
do you walk in love? "Just as Christ also loved you." And
how did Christ love us? He "gave Himself up for us, an
offering and a sacrifice to God." You are never more like
God than when you love, and you are never more like
the love of God than when you forgive.

4. *I forgive to demonstrate real love to the world.*
There's a small but significant word in Ephesians 5:2.
It's the word *walk.* Not only do I imitate God when I
choose to forgive another person, but I am also a perpetual illustration of God's love when a forgiving spirit
characterizes my life, not just on occasion, but *all* the
time. That's the meaning of *walk.* To make something an
everyday part of your life.

5. *I forgive to offer something pleasing to God in worship.* I love the end of verse 2, where Paul says that
Christ "gave Himself up for us, an offering and a sacrifice to God as a fragrant aroma." It was a sacrifice and
offering to God when Christ gave of Himself to forgive
us, and Paul says we're to do the same for other people.
When I forgive someone who has wronged me, I am offering a sacrifice to God. It is an act of worship.

6. *I forgive to guard my walk with God.* The Lord's
prayer recorded in the gospel of Matthew contains a
very hard statement. Remember what Jesus said? "For-

give us our debts, as we also have forgiven our debtors" (Matthew 6:12). That's a weighty prayer. When I pray it, I'm saying, "God, forgive me, but only as much as I forgive other people." That's serious. In fact, the prayer ends with a statement designed to make sure you don't miss the point. Matthew 6:15 says, "If you do not forgive others, then your Father will not forgive your transgressions." An unforgiving spirit hampers my relationship with God. It's that simple.

7. *I forgive to guard my heart from bitterness and evil.* Romans 12:17–20 talks about forgiving, about not seeking revenge, and ends at verse 21 by saying, "Do not be overcome by evil, but overcome evil with good." When I'm unwilling or unable to forgive, who suffers? I do! Whenever I've gotten mad at someone and stayed mad at them, I usually ended up being miserable. But the next time I'd see that person, he wasn't miserable. I could tell by the smile on his face. He'd long since forgotten the whole affair. God says that if you want to stop bitterness from taking root in your heart, learn how to forgive.

8. *Finally, I forgive to help others be restored.* When someone who has offended us realizes what he's done and comes to ask forgiveness, it's not uncommon to hear Christians say, "Sorry, but I just can't forgive you." Paul warns the Corinthian church that when we do that, we can keep people from getting back on track with God. "If any has caused [you] sorrow," he says, "you should rather forgive and comfort him, otherwise such a one might be overwhelmed by excessive sorrow. Wherefore, I urge you to reaffirm your love for him" (2 Corinthians 2:5, 7–8).

HOW DO I FORGIVE?

At this point you may be screaming, "All right, Dale, that's enough motivation! I'm convinced that I should forgive, but my struggle is with the 'how-to's.' In fact, I've tried already and come up short. Is it even in my power to forgive when I'm still angry and hurt?"

The answer is a resounding yes. Forgiveness can be a gift you share even if you're still wounded and hurting. Why? Because at its heart, forgiveness is a *choice*. It's under your control. Let me explain.

Let's start by examining how *God* forgives *us*. Remember we're out to imitate. Hebrews gives us a great place to start.

> [The Holy Spirit] then says, "And their sins and their lawless deeds I will remember no more." Now where there is forgiveness of these things, there is no longer any offering for sin.
>
> Therefore, brethren, since we have confidence to enter the holy place by the blood of Jesus, by a new and living way which He inaugurated for us through the veil, that is, His flesh, and since we have a great priest over the house of God, let us draw near with a sincere heart in full assurance of faith. (Hebrews 10:16b–22a)

Forgiveness: the choice not to get even. This is the heart of forgiveness. It's true of God's forgiveness of us: "Now where there is forgiveness of these things, there is no longer any offering for sin" (v. 18). What's God saying here? That He won't punish you for what you did. He's not interested in getting even. Romans 12:17 says we're to respond the same way to people who've wronged us: "Never pay back evil for evil to anyone." Forgiveness starts by freely giving up the right to get even.

Forgiveness: the choice not to keep score. God says, "Their sins and their lawless deeds I will remember no more" (Hebrews 10:17). Does this mean that God has amnesia? I don't think so. This isn't saying that God can't remember. He's omniscient. He remembers everything. But in the case of forgiven sin, He's not keeping a score sheet somewhere to use against us at some future date. Technically, in fact, this is exactly what Paul means when he says, "Love does not take into account a wrong suffered." In Greek, the words rendered *take into account* mean to keep a ledger. It's an accounting term. In his fine book, *Forgive and Forget*, Lewis Smedes says this:

> When you forgive someone for hurting you, you perform spiritual surgery inside your soul; You cut away the wrong that was done to you. . . . Detach that person from the hurt and you let it go, the way a child opens his hands and lets a trapped butterfly go free.[1]

What a great image of forgiveness. But as you try to get in the habit of not keeping score, keep in mind that God never says it's going to be easy. He just says it'll be worth it. So when you bury the hatchet, don't mark the grave.

Forgiveness: the choice not to demand. The Hebrews text makes it clear that God does not expect us to make another offering for our sin. He's not saying, "All right, I accept you now, but go offer some more things for Me to cover your sins." His offer of forgiveness is unconditional. The entire debt was paid at Calvary. Listen to Romans 11:6: "But if it is by grace, it is no longer on the basis of works, otherwise grace is no longer grace." Forgiveness is a matter of grace, of giving us what we don't deserve, no strings attached.

We need to forgive the same way. When I say, "I'll forgive you *if*," or "I'll forgive you *when*," it's no longer grace. It's a deal. Again, this isn't easy. In fact, to remove consequences from the equation is downright risky. Hence, our fourth and final tip.

Forgiveness: the choice not to withhold love. The challenge here is to invite reconciliation, just as our heavenly Father invites reconciliation. When God says in Hebrews that "their sins and their lawless deeds I will remember no more" (10:17), He's extending forgiveness. When He goes on to say, "Let us draw near with a sincere heart in full assurance of faith" (v. 22*a*), He's going a step further. Now His message is one of reconciliation. He's saying, "I not only want to forgive you. Now I want to encourage you to trust My forgiveness and draw near to Me. Let's get this relationship back on track."

God's grace does this for us, and He wants us to do the same with other people. That is, we're to invite them back into a reconciled love relationship. This is certainly the spirit of Romans 12:18: "If possible, so far as it depends on you, be at peace with all men." As the offended one, we're to take the initiative. Verse 21 of Romans 12 goes on to say that we should "not be overcome by evil, but overcome evil with good." Smedes offers this insight: "You know that forgiveness has begun *when you recall those who hurt you and feel the power to wish them well.*"[2]

When you think of someone who you've "forgiven," are you able to wish them well? You may not want to be their best friend, but do you want good things to come into their lives? That's the point. That's our model for giving grace.

FORGIVING THE TOUGH CASES

OK, now I'm motivated and I'm convinced that the choice is mine. In spite of my feelings, I'm set free to forgive. But are there times when it's just not realistic? What about the tough cases? The deep hurts? There are at least five common reasons we struggle with forgiveness.

I don't forgive because it's not fair. It's just not fair! I don't know about you, but I think I was born with a built-in justice sensor. Maybe it comes from being created in the image of God. When someone has wronged me, a voice inside says, "You know, that guy deserves a payback. It's just not fair for him to get off scot-free." As we saw earlier, Romans 12:17–19 says differently: "Never pay back evil for evil to anyone. . . . Never take your own revenge." The message here is *let God be the judge.* When I'm able to turn the offender over to Him, I can move on. In the end, I know God will be just.

I don't forgive because I just can't forget. This is often the case because consequences remain. Often when people hurt or offend they're quick to extend an apology, but guess what? Apologies don't do away with damages. Many of us live every day with the consequences of past offenses against us. They're with us every morning, which can make it hard to forgive. It's not wise to ignore those feelings. We've also seen that it's not healthy to let them fester inside. One technique I've found helpful is that whenever I recall someone who has hurt me, I use it as an opportunity to pray for that person. It's OK to tell God that it still makes you angry to think about what that person did, but even in the midst of your anger, you can ask Him to help you exercise love by forgiving.

I don't forgive because the offense or consequences are too great. In an article in *The Washington Post,* Elizabeth Pastor wrote of one man's struggle in this area.

> While imprisoned in a Nazi concentration camp, Simon Weisenthal, the Nazi hunter, was confronted by a dying member of the SS seeking to confess to a Jew. "Give me absolution," the man said. Weisenthal would not. He could not. "The crux of the matter is of course the question of forgiveness," Nazi hunter Weisenthal wrote in his 1976 book. "Forgetting is

something that time alone takes care of, but forgiveness is an act of the will, and only the sufferer is qualified to make the decision."[3]

Weisenthal was right. Only the sufferer can decide to forgive. But grace can't stop there. No matter how great the offense, grace chooses to work through the pain and ultimately, as an act of the will, give forgiveness as a gift.

I cannot forgive because I still hurt. This is a paradox, in a sense, because as long as I withhold forgiveness, I prolong the pain. I'm thankful Jesus Christ was able to forgive in the midst of pain. When He was in utter agony, He asked God to forgive those who were causing that pain. You can find freedom if you trust God for the grace and strength to forgive in the midst of pain.

I don't forgive because they haven't changed. Another way of saying this is that they haven't acknowledged their sin or asked for my forgiveness. How can I forgive someone like that? I have to believe Evander Holyfield struggled in this area after Mike Tyson's quick public apology for biting a chunk out of Holyfield's ear in that 1997 title bout. Even if an apology never comes, or sounds insincere, we can still forgive, because forgiveness is a step you take alone. Restoration of a relationship, on the other hand, takes two. Don't confuse the two. If your forgiveness has to wait for full repentance, it may never come, which means you're stuck. You can't move on. Choose to forgive, though, and you're free to leave the pain behind. If restoration follows, all the better.

HOW SHOULD I RECEIVE FORGIVENESS?

For our discussion of "love does not take into account a wrong suffered" to be complete, we have to walk around to the other side of the issue and ask the question, "How should I receive forgiveness?" If more of us understood the biblical perspective on this point, the act of forgiving would become much easier for all of us. It is found, once again, in Hebrews.

This short text spells out where our hearts and heads should be when we're seeking forgiveness. Three simple statements say it all.

1.Come with a humble heart, seeking mercy, not grace. "Let us draw near with a sincere heart in full assurance of faith, having our hearts sprinkled clean from an evil conscience and our bodies washed with pure water" (Hebrews 10:22).

2. Come with a repentant heart, eager to change. "Let us hold fast the confession of our hope without wavering, for He who promised is faithful" (Hebrews 10:23).

3. Come with a loving heart, ready to work at the relationship. "Let us consider how to stimulate one another to love and good deeds, not forsaking our own assembling together, as is the habit of some, but encouraging one another; and all the more as you see the day drawing near" (Hebrews 10:24–26).

How much easier forgiveness is to give when the one seeking it comes like this. How much easier to give grace when mercy is all that's expected. How much easier to be patient and wait for restoration when there's actually eagerness to change. How much easier to join in the restoration process when it's obvious that a healthy relationship has once again become a priority.

LOUIS ZAMPERINI

Forgiving is hard work, but clinging to anger and bitterness is far more difficult. The entire world saw this contrast during the 1998 Winter Olympics in Nagano,

Japan. Between coverage of the various events, the media reported on a host of human-interest stories during those games. One was the saga of Louis Zamperini.

In 1936 Zamperini was a nineteen-year-old trouble-making kid from Torrence, California, who discovered he had a knack for running. He won the first high school race he ever ran, set a new world record for the high school mile at the 1934 California state finals, and qualified for the Olympics the second time he ran 5,000 meters. Due to inexperience, he came up short at the '36 Olympics, finishing eighth. Not one to quit easily, Zamperini set his sights on the 1940 games in Tokyo, Japan, to redeem himself. World War II came first.

Zamperini entered the military, became a bombardier, and was posted to Hawaii. On May 26, 1943, he and eleven other men set off on an ill-fated rescue mission over the Pacific. Their plane lost power and crashed in the ocean, killing nine of the crewmen. Zamperini and the other two survivors climbed into a tiny life raft with a few chocolate bars and half a dozen cans of water. Forty-seven days and two thousand miles later two of them crawled out onto the sandy beach in the Marshall Islands, too weak to walk.

The Japanese occupied that island, and Zamperini ended up in a POW camp under the "care" of Sgt. Mutsuhiro Watanabe, a sadistic psychopath the prisoners nicknamed "the Bird," who was so violent that even the Japanese NCOs hated him. Despite suffering months of brutality at Watanabe's hands in two different camps, Zamperini lived to see the Japanese surrender and returned home after the war. Tormented by nightmares featuring "the Bird," he obsessed on the thought of killing his former captor and may have died an alcoholic if not for God's intervention via a young evangelist named

Billy Graham, who came to Los Angeles for a crusade. Zamperini heard Graham preach and was born again.

Zamperini's faith brought with it peace and removed the hatred and bitterness that had been consuming him. Ministry became such a passion that he returned to Japan, met with many of his former captors and forgave them—all but Watanabe, who had disappeared. Fast-forward to Nagano and the 1998 Olympics. Zamperini has been invited to carry the Olympic torch through the streets, and he uses the opportunity to invite Watanabe, now a wealthy, retired life insurance salesman, to meet with him. Watanabe refuses. Asked by a television announcer what he would have said if the two had been able to meet, the now eighty-one-year-old Zamperini speaks with a slight smile.

"I wanted to face him and tell him right to his face that I forgave him," he says. "I wanted to add some salve to the wound."

NOTES

1. Lewis Smedes, *Forgive and Forget* (New York: Pocket, Simon & Schuster, 1984), 27.
2. Ibid., 29.
3. Elizabeth Pastor, *The Washington Post;* Smedes describes this incident in *Forgive and Forget,* 126–27.

chapter nine

Love Does Not Rejoice in Unrighteousness but Rejoices with the Truth

LOVE TRAFFICS IN TRUTH

Football has always been a part of my life. One of the lessons I learned early in my career (if a ten-year-old on his first team can be called "beginning a career") was that deception is an essential element of the game. Most casual observers of the sport have no idea how much time and attention is devoted to the art of deception on each play. Every player knows that the element of surprise is always your ally in the midst of battle. The quarterback tries to disguise the snap count to give his guys a jump on the defense, then drops back and fakes a handoff to his running back, hopefully freezing the linebackers for just a moment as they think the back has the ball. As the back plows empty-handed into the defenders, the quarterback again conceals the truth by cradling the ball where it can't be seen as he slides deep into the pocket.

Meanwhile the defense is practicing its own skillful deception as the free safety pretends he's dropping back to defend the pass. In reality he's positioning himself for a blitz up the middle. If he successfully hides his intent, he'll avoid all blockers and cream the quarterback from his blind side. You get the idea—trickery, fakery, and foolery are being employed by nearly every player and coach, offensive and defensive, to assure the success of the play. In football, and most sports for that matter, deception is the name of the game. It's not just about who is most powerful, but who can most effectively pull the wool over the opponent's eyes.

Unfortunately, many people today try the same approach in the game of life. They try to get the upper hand through the careful practice of deception. They learn at an early age to disguise their feelings and create masks they can don at a moment's notice to maintain the image they desire. Lying becomes an easy, often accepted way of playing the game and winning. And winning, ending up on top, is the only thing that matters.

Well, deception may work in sports, but not in life and certainly not in love. Love never deals in deception; it traffics in truth. Our next two attributes of love make this point clear, but they can only be interpreted accurately and applied to our lives appropriately if we examine them in tandem.

> Love . . . does not rejoice in unrighteousness,
> *but* rejoices with the truth.

Which leads us to my personal definitions:

love does not rejoice in unrighteousness • love avoids all sin

love rejoices with the truth • love joyfully partners with the truth

Let's dissect the verse into four primary truths and see what they teach us about love. As we explore the parts, the rich meaning of the whole will come into focus. We will close with a discussion of the loss today of a sense of absolute truth and what that loss means for love.

TRUTH #1
LOVE REJOICES

Until now Paul has been defining love simply by presenting its various components. Love is patient, kind, and so forth. But now he brings love to life. It rejoices with the truth, he says, but not in unrighteousness. So we learn that love has an emotional, motivational side to it. We all get excited about something. Certain things get us out of bed in the morning. And we all have things that leave us unmotivated and unwilling to put forth the effort. The question is, what brings you joy? What's your passion? What is it that you really love?

Well guess what . . . love loves certain things too. Think about it. Love rejoices over some things and not others. Paul says love *loves* truth. In fact, the word for "rejoice with" in Greek is *sunchairo*. It's used in the New Testament to describe what happens when people get together to celebrate. In Luke 15:6 and 9, those searching for lost sheep and coins call together their friends and say, "Rejoice with me!" when they find their lost valuables. Let's throw a party; this is great news! The same word is used in Luke 1:58 to describe the birthday party held after Elizabeth gave birth to John the Baptist. It often refers to like-minded people, family or friends, linking up for a season of celebration. Only in 1 Corinthians 13 is it used of two inanimate subjects—love and truth. It is love that joins arms with its friend truth to rejoice.

Love and truth are soul mates. Truth stimulates love to rejoice. Conversely, when sin and deception are in charge, joy will soon disappear. Let's examine the negative side of this declaration more carefully.

TRUTH #2
LOVE DOES NOT REJOICE IN UNRIGHTEOUSNESS

Love finds no joy in sin. In fact, love avoids sin like the plague. Real love—sacrificial, servant love of a 1 Corinthians 13 sort—has nothing in common with sin. This leads to the definition:

love does not rejoice in unrighteousness • love avoids all sin

When I am compelled by love, I am repelled by unrighteousness. The temptations that used to entice me begin losing their power to draw my heart away from the proper recipient of my affections. Perhaps that is why Jesus declared to His disciples, "If anyone loves Me, he will keep My word" (John 14:23). To love God and walk in disobedience just doesn't make sense. First John 4:10–11 declares that we love God because He first loved us and gave His Son for us, then takes love to the next level by exhorting us to pass it on to others. Recipients of such amazing love and grace dare not keep it to themselves. And the more you give away, the more you receive. I can think of two reasons why love never leads us down the path to sin.

First, love has a conscience and listens. God created a conscience in all of us. This is part of what it means to be created in His image. There is within every living soul an innate knowledge of God and of morality. When man sinned, that image of God was marred, but it wasn't destroyed. James reminds us that even unbelievers are created in God's image (James 3:9). And Paul's letter to the

Romans puts it in plain language.

> For the wrath of God is revealed from heaven against all ungodliness and unrighteousness *of men who suppress the truth in unrighteousness, because that which is known about God is* evident within them; *for God made it* evident to them. *For since the creation of the world His invisible attributes, His eternal power and divine nature, have been clearly seen, being understood through what has been made, so that they are without excuse.* (Romans 1:18–20, emphasis added)

The person without Christ knows the truth but suppresses it. He is drawn to unrighteousness even though he may know in his heart that it's wrong. People do know love intuitively when they see it. The problem is, we find ourselves failing to perform those loving actions we know should be characteristic of our lives. Why? Apart from the power of God and the new birth, mankind can never be what God created him to be. (We'll develop this more fully in the final chapter.) But when we experience new life in Christ and begin to walk in love, we will desire righteousness. That doesn't mean we will be perfect; we'll never be fully Christlike until we are with our Lord Himself in glory. But love has its heart focused on righteousness, not sin. It may find temporary pleasure in sin, but not real joy and happiness.

One of the simplest tests we can apply to the way we treat one another is to ask, "Do I feel guilty for the way I'm acting?" Although we can dull the sharp edge of our conscience, the Spirit of God penetrates our spirits, stimulating our heart with the sting of guilt that says, "Hey, Dale, you just blew it again." I may be getting my way, but I will have no joy or peace when my actions fall short of real servant love.

It's not uncommon for the Spirit of God to take the

Word of God and do surgery on my attitudes, which then affects my actions. Love, on more occasions than I'd like to admit, nudges me out of my cushy old leather recliner and puts the towel of a servant into my hands.

Sundays are anything but a day of rest for me. I pour a lot of energy into my teaching of God's Word to our congregation. I'm up early to review my sermon, pray, and prepare to deliver the fruit of a week of long, prayerful, hard study. Before and after our three services, I'm engaged with people—greeting visitors, fielding questions, counseling, and praying. And I love it! I love face-to-face time with people, so I'm usually one of the last to leave the church on Sunday. By the time I hit the homestead, though, I'm often ready to crash.

It was one such Sunday that love booted me off my throne. I had just taken off my tie, kicked off my shoes, and settled back with the sports section when our younger daughter reminded her mom that she had to be dropped at a friend's home across town. As I listened, the following tape was playing in my head:

> I sure hope Becky doesn't expect me to do this . . . but she sure looks swamped right now with dinner . . . one of the other kids can take her . . . after all I am the pastor and this is *my* big day . . . be cool, Dale, and someone else will take her . . . just lie back and close your eyes . . . that will make Bec feel really guilty about asking you to make the run . . . you've earned this break . . . besides, hundreds of people are planning to hear you deliver your stuff again in a couple of hours . . . surely God wants you refreshed and at your best . . . after all this is *God's Word* and you are God's spokesman . . . eternity demands that you get your rest . . .

Then the still, small voice of God whispered . . . "No way!" At least that was the abridged version of God's message. The longer version sounded something like this:

"Dale, get real and get off your throne and practice what you preach! Becky works just as hard as you on Sunday mornings (Ouch, that one hurt!), and your lazy attitude is sin. Love gets off the throne as King Dale of Burkedom and serves his wife. Besides, don't forget that without Me your sermons aren't worth the . . ."

Well, you get the picture. Love has a conscience and listens.

So often in my marriage I'm unsure of just how to love my wife. Does she need love that is patient, or does she need love that speaks the truth? Does she need love that believes in her, trusts in her, and lets her take care of the problem, or does she need me to love by jumping in to fix it, coming to her rescue? Love listens to God, sincerely desiring to do what is right and righteous in every situation. I have found that slowing down long enough to pray and listen—to God and to my wife—usually lands me on the right track.

Second, love cares about the means as well as the end. So often today we look for shortcuts to a good end. Sometimes those shortcuts take us down a road that God's Word warns us to avoid. Love finds no joy in unrighteousness; therefore, love cares not only for the destination but also for the route we choose to get there. I can't believe some of the dumb things people do in the name of love.

I remember the day in my first church when Sam, or so we'll call him, came in for some counseling. He announced that he was leaving his wife and kids, checking out of the marriage. It wasn't that she had done anything terrible or immoral. In fact, he had a lot of great things to say about this lady. But he had fallen out of love. He wasn't happy any longer. So he just felt that God's will—yes, you read it right—that God's will would be for him to leave and start a new life without his wife and kids. Then the kicker . . . he was convinced it was the "loving thing to do." He had already talked it through with God, and God had assured him this was the loving action to take! We had quite a conversation about God, his message from God, and God's definition of love. His desire to bring peace and joy back to a home in turmoil and strife was a good goal. He knew things couldn't go on the way they were going. He wanted to fix it. But he was choosing an unrighteous path toward a righteous objective.

First Corinthians assures us that love always steers us away from sin, not toward it. Now let's learn from the positive side of the equation.

TRUTH #3
LOVE REJOICES WITH TRUTH (HONESTY)

TRUTH WITH A LITTLE "T"

Good friends, good food, good fellowship, good, godly laughter, and singing all rejoice the soul. We all enjoy a good party, especially when lifelong friends are at our side. Truth is one friend that love enjoys teaming up with for a great time. But what is this truth that is such a necessary compatriot of love? In this case, there are two options. Paul is either referring to *truth* or *Truth*. Catch the difference? The verse may be stating, "Love rejoices with truth, or honesty. It shoots straight and always tells the truth." This is love with a little "t." A second possible interpretation reads, "Love rejoices with the Truth, meaning God's Word. It lives according to Scripture. It confronts sin with the Truth of God's moral law." This is love with a capital "T." When seen in contrast to the first part of the verse, "Love does not rejoice in unrighteousness," both views are acceptable alternatives.

This leads to my definition:

love rejoices with the truth • love joyfully partners with the truth

When we speak of truth with a little "t," we are talking about truth as honesty. This love is honest and lays the truth on the table. If you go back and look at what the apostle Paul taught us about love in the last two chapters, you'll recall that love is not easily angered and it forgives. I believe Paul wanted to be certain his readers wouldn't overreact and sacrifice truth on the altar of grace. That would be a deadly mistake! *Grace and truth* and *love and truth* are not contradictory but complementary. The fact that love is patient, kind, slow to anger, and forgiving could lead some to conclude that it simply ignores all sin or unrighteousness. If someone mistreats or abuses me, disappoints or dishonors me, does love expect me to hurt silently and stuff my feelings? Not at all! This verse balances the tolerance and forgiveness of verse 5 with an equally important call to honest confrontation in verse 6. Love is about giving grace, but never to the exclusion of truth.

Jesus set the pattern for this kind of honesty in love relationships. Although His love for us is unconditional, He never ignores sin. He warns us of the damage it can do to people's lives and their relationship with God. His Word doesn't hesitate to shoot straight on sin. He reveals what grieves, hurts, and even angers Him. He also expresses words of encouragement, support, and confidence. Compliments flow from His throne in heaven to His people on earth when He is proud of their faithfulness. He communicates His expectations to His children so they know where the boundaries are in life. Our Father and His Son challenge us with clear hopes, dreams, and a vision for our future. Clear and honest communication is what truth is all about. That's what love does. If it's a consistent part of how God loves us, surely it's essential for our love relationships as well.

One of the more common problems I encounter in marital counseling is unresolved anger. Mary (again, not her real name) had just about lost all hope of salvaging her marriage. Her husband was at the end of his rope as well. So they did what many couples in crisis do. They agreed to give the pastor a final shot at saving their marriage. They had been to several counselors, one provided by their employer and several recommended by the church, but nothing seemed to help. They couldn't put their finger on the problem, but the symptoms of an emotionally dead marriage were apparent. To their credit, Mary and her husband were really trying to change. They were spending time alone, away from their preschool children, going on dates, giving surprise gifts, trying to serve one another. But for some reason, the emotional side of their relationship remained as cold as winter. Their sexual relationship was unfulfilling and virtually nonexistent for several years.

One day I asked Mary, "Are you sure there isn't something making you angry? You tell me your husband's a great guy, but you just can't feel any love for him. Is there something from your past that's made you really angry, but you never dealt with it?" At first she declared, as before, that nothing was left buried from the past. But then something clicked. Her eyes became wet, her teeth clamped tight, and her face darkened. "There's probably one regret I've never discussed with anyone. I've always hated the fact that Bill and I slept together while we were dating before we were married. I never mentioned it because I figured it was as much my fault as his. I could have said no to his advances, but I loved him—or thought I did—and didn't want to risk losing our relationship. And besides, we did go ahead and get married a few months later. So I thought it was silly for me to feel angry over something that's now years behind us." She hesitated, now looking both ashamed and angry, then glared right at Bill. "I've hated you for not wanting to wait. I've felt like you robbed me of one of my lifelong dreams."

As she broke down in tears, Bill reached over, took her hand, and said these words. "I'm sorry. I never realized it bothered you." Mary, in the guise of forgiveness, had stuffed her true feelings. She had deceived her husband and herself into thinking it was no big thing. Once she was honest and verbalized her hurt, Bill was able to ask to be forgiven. From that day on, Mary and Bill began to heal. Their love could only be rekindled when truth came along to clear out the debris left by unresolved pain.

God's Word, as we saw earlier, demands that we forgive. Ephesians says, "[Forgive] each other, just as God in Christ also has forgiven you" (4:32). But the very same chapter commands, "[Speak] the truth in love, . . . Laying aside falsehood, speak truth each one of you with his neighbor. . . . Be angry, and yet do not sin; do not let the sun go down on your anger, and do not give the devil an opportunity" (vv. 15, 25–27). You see, love rejoices with the truth. Until we learn to be honest with one another, even forgiveness does not always heal the emotional scars of conflict. Truth, though, can accelerate our healing.

The honesty theme is not only found in 1 Corinthians. Throughout the Bible, God's Word pleads with us to tell the truth, the whole truth, and nothing but the truth and warns that anything less will eventually get us into trouble, with God and our loved ones.

He who speaks truth tells what is right, but a false witness, deceit. (Proverbs 12:17)

Note that the opposite of honesty is not just lying, but deceit. A good test of my communication is to ask, "Is this designed to clarify or confuse, to reveal or conceal the truth?" When our words are carefully crafted to be technically accurate while misleading our listener to false conclusions, we are being deceptive. Love speaks to reveal the truth. Proverbs continues this theme and cautions us with this prediction:

Truthful lips will be established forever, but a lying tongue is only for a moment. (Proverbs 12:19)

In the long run, truth is our ally and lies are our enemy. Yes, a lie may rush to your rescue on occasion, but the same deception that keeps you out of hot water for the moment will eventually cook your proverbial goose. Telling the truth is certainly no novel idea, so why do we fudge so often? Perhaps the better question is, When should I make sure my love is partnered with the truth? In four areas we should be especially careful to be truthful.

1. *Love tells the truth even when it hurts.* A maxim I've used for years says it best. "Confession is good for the soul but bad for the reputation." One of the hardest times to be honest is when you know the facts aren't in your favor. When I've blown it and know it, it's tempting to shade the truth just enough to cover my sins or short-

comings. The psalmist delivers real wisdom on this very issue.

> *O Lord, who may abide in Your tent?*
> *Who may dwell on Your holy hill?*
> *He who walks with integrity, and works righteousness,*
> *And speaks truth in his heart....*
> *He swears to his own hurt and does not change.*
>
> *(Psalm 15:1–2, 4)*

The person of integrity will tell the whole truth even if the truth will work against him. He swears to his own hurt, does not change the facts, even when it is to his disadvantage. Interestingly, friends, family, and even work associates are often more willing to forgive and forget when we are honest.

We all occasionally forget to do something we've said we would do. I have a bad habit of getting so caught up in my work at the office that I lose track of the time and come home late. Now Becky is a very patient woman, but at times I've really tested that patience. She works hard to plan a great meal for the Burke tribe and to have it ready to go when I come home. But if I'm not there when the chow is ready, it's nearly impossible for her to hold off the troops. Earlier in our marriage I often came rolling in thirty to forty minutes late without even calling to warn her of my delay. On those occasions I could predict what awaited me. It's what I call the "You're late and didn't even call combo"—cold dinner served by hot wife! Now, in an effort to warm the dinner and cool down the wife, I often shaded the truth with a comment like, "Sorry, I had so much to do today," or, "Sorry, honey, I got a call right before I was ready to leave." Now I may have gotten a call and it may have been a busy day, but the usual facts of the matter were that I blew it. I didn't pay attention to the time or allow for the fact I still had to drive home. I knew it. And guess what? So did she.

I still work long hours and at times arrive home late, but I have learned to give Becky the respect she deserves by calling to warn her of my delays. I've also learned it is far better to walk in, give her a hug, and simply say, "I'm sorry, honey . . . there's no excuse . . . I blew it . . . just didn't pay attention to the time." If I'm honest, even when it hurts, my dinner may still be cold, but the temperature in the room will be far more comfortable.

2. *Love tells the truth* especially *when it's hurting*. Most of us are pretty good at getting the facts straight, but when it comes to feelings, communication grinds to a halt. Some have been told from the time they exited the womb that real men, or even today, real women, don't cry. If you hurt, don't share it.

John Madden was one of the finest coaches ever to pace the sidelines of a National Football League game. I'm sure it was because he played the game so well that he coached with such effectiveness and now announces with such success. So whenever Madden talks football, he says it straight and it's usually worth listening to. Like the time I heard him on a television commercial pitching a new electronic football game that bore his name. Of course his words were written by some advertising copywriter, but they came across as pure Madden.

Each ad in this particular series had Madden expounding on some piece of gridiron lore. On the commercial I saw, he was explaining the right way for a running back or receiver to respond if he got leveled by a defensive back or a linebacker. You know, one of those "hits of the week" that make the highlight reels.

"You just pop back up and look at the guy who hit

you and you laugh," Madden said. The intended message, I guess, would be that despite what it looked like to the rest of the world—that you just got run over by a fully loaded 18-wheeler—the truth is you're the tough guy here. If you're hurting, don't show it! And if you stagger on your way back to the huddle, I guess you pretend it's swagger instead. Maybe that's how some of the NFL's best end-zone celebration dances were invented.

Madden's message was kind of funny, and it probably sold a lot of video games, but in the apostle Paul's playbook, it's lousy theology. You see, when Paul says in verse 6, Love "does not rejoice in unrighteousness, but rejoices with the truth," he's pushing a maxim that's very different from Madden's. Rather than swallowing the pain and pretending you didn't feel it, the message here is that when someone hurts you, you need to let him know. Instead of shoving the pain and the damaged emotions under the table, love has a different response. Love talks honestly about its feelings.

As illustrated earlier by Mary and Bill's story, the failure to identify our pain is dangerous to our emotional health and harmful to the love relationships in life. Here are some tips for correcting this tendency:

- *Name it.* Learn to name the offending action and describe your feelings honestly.
  "When you overlook my opinion, I feel unappreciated."
- *Own it.* Approach your spouse or friend as if the problem is yours.
  "I'm feeling so angry, it's hard for me to talk to you," or
  "It would really help me if we could talk this out."

- *Forgive it.* Offer love and forgiveness unconditionally but honestly.
  "I forgive you, but this is making me angry."

3. *Love tells the truth, expressing its expectations clearly.* One of the things I love most about our heavenly Father is that He never keeps His children in the dark. From the Garden of Eden to the Garden of Gethsemane, from the Ten Commandments to the Great Command-ment, God never stutters when He speaks. He lays out the truth in language we can all understand. The bound-aries are clear and defined. His expectations for our be-havior are repeated again and again in case we didn't quite get it the first time through. Deuteronomy speaks with the clarity of fine crystal,

> *"See, I have set before you today life and prosperity, and death and adversity; in that I command you today to love the Lord your God, to walk in His ways and to keep His commandments and His statutes and His judgments, that you may live and multiply, and that the Lord your God may bless you in the land where you are entering to possess it." (30:15–16)*

Especially in our homes, it is vital that we not sur-prise one another with unspoken expectations. Don't as-sume that your loved ones will intuitively know what you want or need from them. Better to speak those expecta-tions, as God does, clearly and often. I believe strongly that when Adam fell into sin in the garden, whatever an-tennae God had given him for picking up Eve's coded signals were seriously damaged. Even in maturing Christians, the ability to tune in to the opposite gender's unspoken signals is at best minimal and full of static. Take a lesson from the Great Communicator, the Author of Holy Scripture: Say it often; say it clear.

4. *Love tells the truth without destroying others.* You may now be wondering, Does this mean that I should always say exactly what's on my mind? Must I always reveal the whole truth? Again, God's Word provides the balance. Ephesians gives us some guidelines for truth-telling.

> *Let no unwholesome word proceed from your mouth, but only such a word as is good for edification according to the need of the moment, so that it will give grace to those who hear. (4:29)*

Just four verses earlier Paul exhorted us to be more truthful with one another, to not let the sun go down on our anger. Now he gives us the guidelines. Honesty is not a license to kill with our words. It's a permit to build, not to destroy. Here are at least four questions, right out of this text, to ask before you dump the whole truth on those you love.

- *Am I under control?* "Let no unwholesome word proceed from your mouth" assumes you are calling the shots, that you're in command of your tongue and the product it produces. If not, get alone with God and give yourself a chance to gain His perspective on what you should or should not say.
- *Is my motive to edify or build up?* "Only such . . . as is good for edification" reminds me that my motive matters as much as the words I choose. God wants all my words to be constructive, to help and heal rather than to hurt.
- *Is this the right time and place?* "According to the need of the moment" slows me down to make sure the timing is right. Sometimes even the right words, lovingly shared at the wrong time, can cause great damage. Place yourself in the shoes of

the other person and be sure the setting is right for the truth you're about to share.

• *Are my spirit and words full of grace?* "So that it will give grace to those who hear" calls me to clothe my words with love and grace. Remember, grace is giving someone what they do not deserve. Jesus was full of grace and truth. Our truth must partner with grace to emulate the love of 1 Corinthians 13.

If we apply these tests from this one great verse, we'll have no trouble deciding how much truth to deliver at any one time or place. Just remember, love is honest.

TRUTH #4
LOVE REJOICES WITH *THE* TRUTH

TRUTH WITH A CAPITAL "T"

This use of truth refers to the Word of God. Love lives according to Scripture, follows God's moral law, and will confront when necessary. Hence an alternate definition could read:

love rejoices with *the* truth · love confronts with the truth and seeks to live according to Scripture

Consider this text:

For I was very glad when brethren came and testified to your truth, that is, how you are walking in truth. (3 John 3)

Throughout the New Testament "*the* truth" refers to the gospel or Scripture, the divine guide for Christian hope which is the salvation message of Jesus Christ, whereas "walking *in* the truth" means living the Christian life. We can take considerable comfort in the fact that as we're following Jesus' model for responding to unrighteousness and resolving the conflict that arises as a result, we are giving those who watch not just a glimpse of good relational skills, but also an idea of what it looks like when God is at work in His people. This, I have to believe, brings a smile to our heavenly Father's face. It also suggests a supplementary definition for "Love rejoices in the truth," namely, *"Love that rejoices in God's Word and not man's."*

In his second letter to Timothy, Paul summarizes the many roles the truth plays in our everyday lives.

> *All Scripture is inspired by God and profitable for teaching, for reproof, for correction, for training in righteousness; so that the man of God may be adequate, equipped for every good work. (2 Timothy 3:16–17)*

This type of divine guidance is not unlike the automatic pilot on an aircraft. Once the destination is programmed in, an automatic course correction is made if the plane veers off course. To work effectively, however, the autopilot must have a "true north" by which to get a bearing and gauge the plane's location. As children of God, we do well to remember that God and His Word set our true north. Scripture provides the guide by which we can gain our bearings and make course corrections as we navigate through the difficult passages of life.

ABSOLUTE TRUTH

Any discussion of truth in relationships today must address one more issue. As the twentieth century winds down, the notion of absolute truth—of moral rights and moral wrongs—has become passé for many people. Make that most people. "Most Americans believe that all truth is relative," says George Barna, researcher and author of the 1995 book *Generation Next*. Among the statistics to back up Barna's words: 57 percent of teenagers believe that sometimes it's necessary to lie.[1]

If we're going to get serious about loving, we have to understand the insidious implications of this shift away from moral absolutes toward moral relativism. This shift is the logical consequence of a culture that has bought into a worldview that places men and women at the center instead of the One who belongs there—God. Humanism is the most apropos name for such a view, and the digression it triggers spells slow but certain calamity if left unchecked. It goes like this. If people are at the center of everything, then morality becomes entirely subjective. Under this view, if I like monogamous heterosexual relationships and you like some other kind, neither of our preferences is right or wrong. There is not "truth," at least none I can be sure of. What I like is right for me, and likewise for you. Essentially, nothing is absolutely right or absolutely wrong.

What makes this view so insidious is that as it has taken root over the past thirty or so years, it has redefined more than just truth—what's right or wrong. It has also changed the way you and I are expected to respond to others' views of truth. The key word in most any discussion of moral choices is *tolerance,* but, oh, how the definition of this word has changed. Whereas once it meant allowing another's behavior without accepting it, today tolerance is being defined as not only accepting but moving over and making room at the table for the behavior, honoring it as an equal, in some cases even applauding it. The current approach to homosexuality is the most prominent example of this type of thinking.

Where this moral shift upsets our quest for love is

precisely in the realm of how we respond to unrighteousness. Under biblical morality, since there are stan-
dards of behavior, there are also ample opportunities to
shine the light of Truth into the dark corners of unrighteousness. This is called confrontation, and when done
in love, as we have seen, it can lead to genuine rejoicing.
With relative morality, it's a different story. Since right
and wrong have been blended to become a sea of gray
areas, we're called to condone rather than confront, so
love has no room to operate. Such a system essentially
denies Truth, and in the process forces love out of the
picture. The hard truth is, *if I can't tell you the Truth, I
can't truly love you.*

This distinction is expressed in John's description of
Jesus near the beginning of his gospel when he says,
"The Word" (Jesus) is "full of grace and truth" (John
1:14). The Word is not full of one or the other, not filled
with grace but lacking truth, or filled with truth but
lacking grace. It's full of both. The danger today is to be
strong on one and not the other. To express godly love,
we must keep a firm grip on both. The day I compromise the Truth I contaminate my love.

This leads us back to the autopilot mentioned earlier. Within each one of us is a moral compass. Like the
autopilot, to operate correctly and lead us where we
want to go, that compass needs a "true north" to guide
it. Where do we find our true north? God in His Word
gives us our bearings. Find God and you will discover
love. Deny Him and His ways and, as the pop song says,
you'll always be looking for love in all the wrong places.
I'm reminded of Jesus' response when Thomas asked
Him how to get to heaven. "I am the way, and truth, and
the life," Jesus said.

Love finds no joy in hanging out with sin but loves to

party with the truth. Whether that's truth with a capital "T"—God's Word—or truth with a little "t"—truthfulness—love and truth are like best friends. You'll always find them together.

Why does love lay Truth on the table? It only makes sense. Truth laid love on the table first.

NOTE

1. George Barna, *Generation Next: What You Need to Know About Today's Youth* (Ventura, Calif.: Gospel Light, Regal, 1995).

chapter ten

Love Bears All Things, Believes All Things

LOVE BEARS ALL THINGS

I have a habit. When I'm driving in the car, I love listening to music and using the rings on my fingers to tap along with the tune. I'll tap on any hard surface within reach. For some reason I like the way it sounds. Those clangy taps kind of enhance the instrumentation. My older daughter, Beth, disagrees. I know this because she tells me whenever we're riding in the car together and my fingers start tapping. "Dad, would you just stop it!" is what she says. "It really bugs me when you do that."

I looked up "bug" in the dictionary and found no reference to finger tapping. Not specifically. But it did say that to bug is to do "anything that annoys or pesters." One question springs to mind. Are bugs called bugs because they bug us, or do we say something bugs us because bugs bug us? I have no idea, and it doesn't matter, but I know that my finger tapping bugs Beth. It irritates her to no end.

When Paul says that love "bears all things," I'm sure

he was talking about trials that are more threatening than minor irritants, although irritants could easily be one of the categories he had in mind. Other irritants include the imperfect and irregular aspects of life. More telling than the specific items on any list of things that love might bear is the intent behind love's forbearance. This intent is reflected in the Greek word that we read here as "bear." It's the word *stego*.

In a literal usage it means to roof over or cover something. It was used for covering something to protect it from rain or water or for thatching a roof to keep the water out. But in a more figurative sense, it came to refer to covering with silence or enduring with patience. It's used in 1 Thessalonians 3:1 and 3:5 as Paul declares that after waiting and waiting for news from the church at Thessalonica, only when he "could bear it no longer," he sent Timothy to check on their progress. To bear up under adverse circumstances for the welfare of others, that's real *stego*, that's real love. So let's try a working definition of this expression of forbearing love.

bears all things · love that hangs tough

The imperfect things of life are the incomplete, defective, flawed things that happen to me simply because other people are flawed and imperfect (just like me). Irregular things are those that are out of the ordinary. Not in the instruction book. Unexpected. Love, we're being told here, can handle these kinds of things. It doesn't cut and run when they crop up or start to pile up.

Tolerating imperfections. The capacity to bear all things is obviously of value to the one we love, but it goes well beyond that. "Let your gentle spirit be known to all men," Paul writes later on to the Philippian church (4:5). In other words, work at building a reputation for this type of tolerant behavior. He's not talking about tolerating sinful behavior, but rather behavior which isn't right or wrong but simply a matter of preference. Neither is he talking about grinning and bearing it. The attitude Paul's looking for here is more a matter of service with a smile. If my tolerance of another's imperfections brings a frown rather than a smile to my face, I'm not bearing all things. You might say I've become unbearable myself.

Accepting personal differences. Of course, different things bug different people. Personality differences are often the root cause. Administratively gifted people can get frustrated with creative types, and vice versa. People who like to do things one way may infuriate folks who like to do them another. Whether it's habits, tardiness, or a certain way of talking, life has plenty of irritants to throw your way.

Overlooking selfishness. I've found that one of the toughest "things" to bear is when someone seems to be taking advantage of me. It's hard to love a guy who doesn't seem to be pulling his weight at work and expects me to pick up the slack. It's hard to love my kids when selfishness seems to be their driving motivation. It's hard to love fellow Christians who expect me to say yes every time they need my help even though my schedule sometimes demands that I say no. I read a great story the other day that reminded me of the importance of keeping a smile nearby when occasions like this arise. The title was "Why Am I So Tired." It was written by that most famous of authors, Anonymous. It goes like this.

For a couple of years I've been blaming my fatigue on poor blood, lack of vitamins, dieting, and a dozen other maladies, but now I've found out the real reason I'm so tired. I'm tired because I'm overworked. Here's why. The population of this country is about 237 million people. 104 million are retired, which leaves 133 million to do all the work. 85 million are in school, which leaves 48 million to do all the work. Of this number, 29 million are employed by the federal government, which leaves 19 million to do all the work. There are over 4 million in the armed forces, which leaves 15 million to do all the work. Of that number, 14.8 million work for state and city governments, which leaves 200,000 of us to do all the work. On an average day, 188,000 people are in America's hospitals, which leaves 12,000 of us to do all the work. Since 11,998 people are in prison, that leaves just the two of us to do all the work, and you're listening to me!

Cute story. And it makes the point well. When we're talking about behavior other than sin, "love bears all things" and even does it with a smile.

LOVE BELIEVES ALL THINGS

In his commentary on 1 Corinthians 13, Matthew Henry makes a wonderfully wise statement. "All charity is apt to make the best of everything; it will judge well, and believe well. And yet, when in spite of inclination, it cannot believe well of others, it will hope well." This is the spirit of Paul's words in this section of his love letter. The word he uses is one of the most common terms in the New Testament. The word is *pisteuo,* and each of the 218 times it's used, this word means either to have faith in, to believe in, or to trust. Hence, our definition:

believes all things · love that communicates confidence

Nothing builds up a loved one more quickly than a well-timed, "I believe in you!" These are words with power, and when we wield them we slay the demons of defeatism. Conversely, nothing deflates more quickly than to cast doubt at the moment of commitment with a thoughtless question like, "Do you really think you can do that?" The difference between these statements is that the negative tears people down while the positive builds them up. That's at the heart of Paul's choice of words here. By communicating confidence, love gets into the construction business . . . the business of building up people.

Love that "believes all things" is needed more at certain times in our lives than others. A friend once told me of an incident that occurred when he was younger which left him in desperate need of someone to believe in him. He was a young college student at the time, struggling to work his way through school. Due to a fluke series of circumstances at work, he got fired. While my friend felt he was innocent in the matter and had therefore been wrongly dismissed, he just couldn't bring himself to face his boss and tell his side of the story. He needed someone to stand beside him, to speak on his behalf. And that's exactly what the father of the family he was living with at the time did. He put a reassuring arm around my friend's shoulder, expressed confidence in his integrity, and encouraged him to go have that talk with his boss. "I'll go with you," this man said, "and I'll stand right beside you." He actually went a step further and vouched for this young man's character. Unfortunately, he didn't get his job back. But the good news is he lost neither his dignity nor his self-confidence, because someone showed love by believing in him.

Checking the Bible for insights, I've found four facts about people who excel at building others up with words of confidence. They're found in 1 Corinthians 12, the chapter just before Paul's love letter.

1. *People builders know their mission is to be focused on others.* This appears in verses 4 to 7, which speak of

the various gifts God gives to His church. After listing these gifts, Paul says why they're given: "for the common good" (v. 7). We are able to build up others because God gives all of us gifts for that very purpose. They're different gifts to be sure, but all are given for the same mission. What makes the use of these gifts doubly encouraging is that when we use them to bolster others whose spirits are sagging, we end up bolstering our own sense of well-being in the process. There's nothing like making a positive difference in other people's lives to energize your own.

2. *People builders know that God is the source of all ministry.* They recognize that the power to love like this comes from the Spirit of God. "But one and the same Spirit works all these things, distributing to each one individually just as He wills" (v. 11). This statement follows a listing of gifts given "for the common good." What it teaches is that I can't generate the power to exercise these "building-up" gifts. Only as I walk with God am I enabled, by the Spirit's power, to build up other people. It's important as I seek to really encourage those around me that I stay dependent on God and remind others to do the same. My confidence in people is ultimately based in my confidence in God, the Giver of every good gift.

3. *People builders don't tend to operate solo.* They're vitally connected to a body. That's their base of operations. "For even as the body is one and yet has many members," Paul writes, "and all the members of the body, though they are many, are one body, so also is Christ. For by one spirit we were all baptized into one body. . . . For the body is not one member, but many" (vv. 12–14). The point here is that the church is a complex organism, a body, and when you come to Christ,

you become part of that body. It is from this strong base of operations that you're able to do anything of significance, including the vital work of building people. The key to being ready to love is being connected to a body of believers.

It's true that encouraging and communicating confidence can be done one-on-one. At times that is the best venue. But other times these vital signs of body life are better expressed in a group setting. The preacher says that "a cord of three strands is not quickly torn apart" (Ecclesiastes 4:12). Some people need to hear "you can do it" multiple times, from a multitude of people, before they can believe it.

4. *People builders know they are both needed and needy.* This final fact reminds us that loving is a reciprocal proposition. "If the foot says, 'Because I am not a hand, I am not a part of the body,' it is not for this reason any the less a part of the body. And if the ear says, 'Because I am not an eye, I am not a part of the body,' it is not for this reason any the less a part of the body. If the whole body were an eye, where would the hearing be? If the whole were hearing, where would the sense of smell be? But now God has placed the members, each one of them, in the body, just as He desired" (vv. 15–18). The fact is, I am needed. And the fact also is that I am needy. Each one of us, when we become part of Christ's body, bring something that others in the body need. It's the capacity to "build into" others, to help them along in their walk of faith. And you can count on days coming when you'll be the one needing the reassuring hand on your shoulder that says, "I believe in you!"

Expressions of confidence such as this can shape us for life. When I was a high school senior I actually began to preach in some small churches, usually on "Youth

Sunday." And when I say "small," I'm talking about a group of churches so small that they had to share one pastor. At times I'd bring along six or seven friends to lead the music and share testimonies, and on occasion we actually doubled a church's attendance. One day, though, I had an opportunity to address a much larger audience. It was a big youth rally held in our high school gymnasium, and although I'd prepared hard, I was understandably nervous. Fact is, I was scared to death.

Much to my surprise, God graciously worked through my weakness (isn't that just like Him?) to move hearts to Himself. After I'd spoken, a man came up and told me that he believed God had uniquely gifted me to preach. Now to fully appreciate the impact of this statement, keep in mind that at age seventeen my "sermons" were rough . . . *real* rough . . . but this man saw something worth noting in that raw material. He believed in me, and he communicated it. God used that encouragement and affirming words of others along the way to set the course for my life.

These four facts taken together create a significant section of our job description as people committed to loving others. I've tried to illustrate this role in the diagram on the next page. On the far left side is an atheist. To the far right is a mature Christian. Along the way from left to right you see one walking toward the cross, coming to faith in Christ. There's another looking dejected, facing the other way. That may be you, or maybe you're the third figure. He's interested, going to church, but pretty much in a holding pattern. And there are the people on the right side of the cross. They're Christians, but some are walking toward maturity, others are headed the other way. Some are just standing in place, kind of stuck. A few are discouraged, even downtrodden. If you take the whole continuum, it represents the whole of humanity. Each of us and everyone we meet falls somewhere along that line. And believing in people who cross our part of the line each day is one way we can help those people move a step closer to mature faith. Our challenge is to love by encouraging each person God brings into our life. We may not be able to take them all the way to maturity, but we can meet them where they're at and encourage them to move in the right direction, one step at a time.

Faith in Christ

Total Unbelief

Spiritual Maturity

Where are you on that continuum? Where is your wife or husband? Your kids? Your grandchildren? Coworkers? Your best friend? Your neighbor across the street? Do you know enough about their lives to know where they are in their walk and to know how you might encourage them to take another step in the right direction? Maybe it's time to find out. Love says, "I believe in you." Love that communicates confidence is love that moves people closer to the Savior.

chapter eleven

Love Hopes All Things, Endures All Things

LOVE HOPES ALL THINGS

What's the quickest way to kill the human spirit? It's been said that a man can live forty days without food, about three days without water, about eight minutes without air . . . but only about one second without hope. When hope is gone, desperation quickly moves in for the kill. Ask anyone who has watched a dream die. Or promised help never come. Or children turn in defiance and walk away.

It is evident from his letter that Paul understood both our needs and love's capacity to meet them. He knew from personal experience, for example, that hope is the best antidote for despair. He expresses this truth almost poetically in his letter to the Romans.

Now we who are strong ought to bear the weaknesses of those without strength and not just please ourselves. Each of us is to please his neighbor for his good, to his edification. (Romans 15:1–2)

What follows in the chapter is a bold treatise on an other-centered lifestyle that is consistent with the pattern he presents in his entire epistle. The heart of this treatise beats in verse 13:

> *Now may the God of hope fill you with all joy and peace in believing, so that you will abound in hope by the power of the Holy Spirit.*

This hope, *elpis* in Greek, is a word full of confident expectation. Its verbal form, *elpizo,* means to expect or anticipate with pleasure and confidence. Hope knows where it is headed. It knows the outcome of the game before it even begins. It knows the final act before the curtain is even raised. Hope may be based on God's promises for tomorrow, but love knows it's needed for today. Therefore, love looks for opportunities to deliver wherever and whenever it's in short supply.

Love is full of hope because it sees the future through the eyes of God and helps others do the same. Love knows that with God in the formula, we should never quit, never give in to despair. Hope-filled love never lets defeat have the last word or despair the final moment. So, with this in mind, let me offer the following definition:

hopes all things • love that is optimistic and smiles at the future

The $64 question today, as it has always been, is simply this: When joy and peace are flagging, how do we communicate hope to resuscitate a broken heart? After all, we don't have to wait long for circumstances to come along that offer little cause for hope. In my experience, finding hope is a matter of focusing, or refocusing, our attention on the Source of our hope and the evidence that proves our hope is not ill-spent. We do well to direct our focus and the focus of others to three areas.

1. *Focus on the person of God.* When dark days or broken dreams blur the blessings of life, a refresher course on the Author of life can work wonders for our sagging spirits. Proverbs says that "hope deferred makes the heart sick" (Proverbs 13:12). If your heart is sick, may I suggest the following prescription? Each day for a week, starting on Monday, take the doses of Scripture listed below. Or stretch them out, dwelling on each Scripture reference for a day. Beside each day's dosage I've listed the active ingredients of God's character that the verses for that day contain. Savor each one and be reminded of why you can "abound in hope." If you focus on the unchanging, reliably predictable, incomprehensible, ever-present person of God, hope will be restored.

WHO IS GOD?

Monday	1. Romans 11:33–36	My wisdom and judgment
	2. Psalm 116:1–2	My listener
	3. Psalm 48:1	Great and majestic
	4. Psalm 103.8	Compassionate, gracious
	5. Ephesians 6:11	My armor
Tuesday	6. Psalm 23	My shepherd
	7. Psalm 46	My refuge
	8. Philippians 2:5–6	Servanthearted
	9. Isaiah 9:6	Counselor, Mighty God, Father
	10. Psalm 139	Omniscient, omnipresent (unlimited in knowledge and always present)
Wednesday	11. Romans 9:14–15	Sovereign
	12. Philippians 2:8	Obedient
	13. Psalm 11:7	Righteous
	14. Psalm 145:8–10	Loving, slow to anger, good
	15. 2 Timothy 3:16	Teacher

Thursday	16. John 1:14	Incarnate
	17. 2 Corinthians 5:9–10	Judge of believers
	Romans 11:22	
	18. Jonah 4:2; 1 John 1:9	Forgiving
	19. Psalm 103:1–5	Healing
	20. Job 19:25	Redeemer
Friday	21. John 1:9	Light
	22. Romans 11:33–36	Focus of all, above all
	23. Hebrews 4:15; 7:24	Personal, sympathetic High Priest
	24. Ephesians 2:1–7	Merciful
	25. Genesis 1	Creative, Creator
Saturday	26. Revelation 1:8	Alpha and Omega
	27. 2 Corinthians 1:3–5	Concerned, caring
	28. Deuteronomy 33:27	Eternal
	29. Psalm 100:5	Faithful
	30. Philippians 1:2	Father
	31. Isaiah 26:4	Rock

2. *Focus on the promises of God.* When Abraham's hope began to fail him, Paul told the Romans, he regained it by turning his attention to God's promises. "In hope against hope he believed, . . . yet, with respect to the promise of God, he did not waver in unbelief, but grew strong in faith, giving glory to God" (Romans 4:18*a*, 20). Here again we find in the Scriptures a strong prescription for restoring hope. It is to remind yourself of God's promises and thank Him for them.

No matter how reliable a person is purported to be, it means nothing to me unless that person has made promises to me as an individual and subsequently kept those promises. The Rockefeller clan may be wealthy, but that doesn't help my poverty or give me hope in a financial crisis—unless I'm in the Rockefeller family or a friend they've promised to support. The good news for us is that God has spoken words of promise. I'd suggest starting with the following dozen hope-boosting promises.

TWELVE REASONS TO HAVE HOPE!

You are always with me	Hebrews 13:5
You love me as Your child	Romans 8:15–16
You gave Your only Son for me	Romans 8:32
Your power is available to me	Philippians 4:13
You can do anything	Ephesians 3:20
You know everything about me	Matthew 6:8
You will supply all my needs	Philippians 4:19
Your grace is sufficient for me	2 Corinthians 12:9
You work all things for good	Romans 8:28
You use trials to produce maturity	James 1:2–4
You use trials to reach others	Philippians 2:15
Your will is good and perfect	Romans 12:2

3. *Focus on progress, not perfection.* Sometimes the culprit who pulls the plug on our hope is ourselves. We ratchet our expectations up way too high and keep expecting them to be reached, with the result that we often miss significant progress that's being made. Once again, Paul provides an alternative focal point to draw our attention back to reality, where it belongs. It's that familiar text found in his letter to the Philippians.

> *Finally, brethren, whatever is true, whatever is honorable, whatever is right, whatever is pure, whatever is lovely, whatever is of good repute, if there is any excellence and if anything worthy of praise, dwell on these things. (Philippians 4:8)*

Is the glass half full or half empty? Our perspective has a major impact on our attitude. Often in counseling, the first challenge is to restore hope. To help the person see that the glass isn't empty. I begin by pointing people to the person and promises of God, but I also try to help them see even the slightest hints of progress. Despite their tendency to focus on what's lacking, I start to steer the conversation toward progress that's been made. It's not always easy. Sometimes we have to go back six months to see improvement. Hope doesn't just focus on today, it looks into the future and envisions a new day. If I can help them see some progress, it brightens their hope for the future.

For couples, another technique is to make a list of ten things each appreciates about the other and pray twice a day through that list. For parents, a temptation can be to blow the negatives out of proportion, to focus on our kids' shortfalls instead of their progress. In doing so, we run the risk of making our kids angry or exasperating them, both of which the Bible admonishes us to avoid (Ephesians 6:4; Colossians 3:21).

If these three prescriptions for healing the hopeless heart are going to work, they must be taken with two reminders. First, *remember that present circumstances are a poor gauge of your long-range prognosis.* Don't let current circumstances destroy your long-term dreams. Second, *remember that hope, like the love that delivers it, is not primarily a feeling.* It's a choice to believe in the person of God, who delivers on His promises. Choose to welcome hope based on what you know—about the person and promises of God, about the progress you've made—and the feeling won't be far behind.

LOVE ENDURES ALL THINGS

The word rendered "endures" here is the same Greek word James uses when he says, "Blessed is a man who perseveres under trial" (James 1:12). The *New International*

Version, in fact, translates the phrase in 1 Corinthians as "love . . . always perseveres." The word is *hupomeno*, which literally means "to remain in a place instead of leaving it," or "to stay behind."

In Greek, *meno* means to stay in a given place or a given state. In its more literal usage it is translated with a variety of terms, such as *abide, live, continue, stay, dwell,* or *tarry*. Our term adds the primary preposition *hypo*, usually translated among, in, or under. The result is endurance or perseverance, the willingness to remain under or stay in adverse conditions.

The dictionary definition gives us even further insight. Perseverance, it says, means to "persist in spite of difficulty." It's as if Paul is putting before us the image of a competitor who won't give up. So let's try this for a definition.

endures all things · love that is willing to suffer

Have you ever watched the Ironman Triathlon staged in Hawaii each year? If ever there was a picture of perseverance, it's the scene at the end of the course about eight hours after the top runners have crossed the finish line. For most people this race is not about winning. It's about finishing. Race rules, however, require that a competitor finish in eighteen hours or less for his or her effort to qualify. So the emotion runs deep the longer the race wears on, and it engulfs the dwindling crowd of spectators during those magical minutes, long after the sun has set, when each of the final qualifiers grinds out those final anguished steps to the wire. I'll never forget the time a couple of years ago when one of these "persevering" ironpeople, a sixty-nine-year-old woman, came into the camera's view. Hunched over in backbreaking agony, well past the point of either fatigue or exhaustion, she refused to stop shuffling one lead foot past the other. Only after those blistered feet had carried this lady across the finish line did they collapse with the rest of her body into an oddly triumphant heap of misery.

Love is well illustrated by the combined efforts of those lingering spectators and the final finishers, but of course it is much more than that. The endurance required in relationships seldom has a finish line waiting to be crossed and a crowd waiting to cheer you on. There is no adrenaline rush from the competitive nature of the opportunity to endure. More often the endurance required in relationships demands that you hang on in the face of unjust or unfair treatment. Note Peter's use of the word in this part of his first letter.

> For what credit is there if, when you sin and are harshly treated, you endure it with patience? But if when you do what is right and suffer for it you patiently endure it, this finds favor with God. (1 Peter 2:20)

This is exactly what Jesus' love for us prompted Him to do, and we follow His example when our love for others challenges us to endure on their behalf.

A willingness to persist through pain, to suffer for another, is no easy assignment. And why is it that I often struggle most in this area when it comes to those I love the most? Given the difficulty of the task, I think the hardest question to answer when endurance is the order of the day is *how*. How do I put shoe leather on this aspect of my faith? The best answer I've found is to avoid letting unrelated issues convince me to give up prematurely. Three likely ones come to mind. Think of them as the three F's of failure.

1. *It's not feasible.* The issue here is really convenience. You can count on it. Endurance will put you to

work right in the midst of busy schedules or bad circumstances. There will be 101 reasons to say, "Not now"
or "Maybe later." Don't be fooled into thinking that endurance runs on your timetable. It usually runs over
your schedule and asks you to run right along with it.

2. *It's not fun.* This one seems obvious, but it has to
be singled out. We don't like to be shoved outside of our
comfort zone. We like our leisure, our recreation, our
hobbies, our sleep. Endurance seldom sleeps, ignores
alarm clocks, and never takes a vacation. When it comes
knocking at your door, don't let your desire for pleasure
keep you from dealing with the pain. I love that line in
the movie *Hoosiers,* when the new basketball coach responds to one of the player's complaints about the inten-
sity of practice. "My practices," the coach said, "are not
designed for your enjoyment."

3. *It's not fair.* This one is the most likely to knock you
off the track before you ever start the race. There's
enough bad track between poor decisions and bum circumstances to convince you the effort isn't worth it. But
when love hears the words "This is a no-win situation," it
responds to the challenge rather than resigning itself to
defeat. It is willing to work toward healing and wait for
justice. When the situation seems unfair, don't run with
the opinion of the crowd. Blaze a new trail if you have to.

The sport of cross-country running is a great model
for love that "endures all things." Watching my son, Paul,
in this sport was a live demonstration of endurance.
Training for each week's 3.1-mile race is rigorous and
painful, with no one except your teammates there to
spur you on. Come race day, the dynamics beg you to
give up. Everyone starts together, but soon it seems that
it is you against the course, alone. As the race grinds on
you're sucking for wind, feeling fire in your leg muscles,

and, in many cases, fighting nausea. The twin demons of "walking" and "quitting" lurk around every bend, halfway up every hill. But cross-country runners endure to the end. Why? It isn't just to come in first place. Few runners can hope for that outcome. No, individual runners endure for the good of the team. The first five finishers determine which team will win a meet, and every runner who endures knows that the payoff for all the pain just might be a victory for the team.

It only makes sense. Once love has made up its mind to bear all things, believe all things, and hope all things, the best way to express those convictions is to endure.

part three
the permanence
of **LOVE**

Paul has made a strong case, hasn't he? First, if we want to really live, then love has to be the number one priority in our lives. Settling for less reduces our best efforts to the musical equivalent of a "noisy gong or a clanging cymbal." And second, despite the flowery descriptions of poets and playwrights, love . . . godly love . . . has concrete characteristics that we can understand and apply to our relationships. It isn't all guesswork. One question, though, not only remains but demands an answer. It's the question of staying power. Will this love last?

Paul's response is concise and emphatic. Just as God stretched the rainbow across the heavens to declare His promise to Noah and company of permanent protection from any future global flooding, so He stretches His love across time and eternity with the assurance to you and me that "when the perfect comes," love will usher it in. And once on the scene, this love will "abide." Of all God's marvelous gifts, this is the one that will neither disappear nor even diminish. On the contrary, it will come clearer the closer we come to it.

What we're talking about here, then, is a love that is unlike any you've ever known. In a world rubbed raw by hatred, worn out by war, and frightened by the futility of temporary solutions, Paul offers an alternative, A Love That Never Fails.

chapter twelve

Love
Never Fails

PUTTING LOVE TO THE TEST

When you add up the lengths to which love is willing to go in 1 Corinthians 13, verses 1 through 3, and all the attributes of love listed in verses 4 through 7, the result is a resource that will never let you down. Never fail you. With love, *God's* love, you're equipped to make a positive difference in other people's lives.

So often we are tempted to try another approach to solving our problems, to use our logic to arrive at new ways of expressing love. But God concludes His list of attributes by declaring, "Love never fails!"

The Greek word used in this phrase appears eighty-five times in the New Testament, and only here is it translated "fail." The typical translation for *pipto* is "to fall," not "to fail." What God is saying is that choosing to love, as 1 Corinthians 13 defines love, will never let you down. It's always the right thing to do. Just do it! . . . and you won't be disappointed. So our working definition is as follows:

never fails • love that works, even when put to the test

God is not saying that love always delivers the result you desire. First Corinthians 13 isn't even promising that love delivers the result God desires. As we extend love to someone, it may be rejected. It may even cause more pain, since honesty and confrontation sometimes lead to increased conflict. But we need to remember, especially when tempted to take an unloving approach to solving our problems, that love never fails. It stands and does not fall under the test of real life.

I'm reminded of God's counsel in Romans 12:18. "So far as it depends on you, be at peace with all men." Great advice and encouragement to keep our relationships healthy and be sure our conflicts are resolved. Romans 12 is a great chapter on loving as a lifestyle, but verse 18 makes it clear that we can only do so much. We can forgive. We can choose not to seek revenge. We can offer love and forgiveness all by ourselves, but it takes two to experience reconciliation. The other person can reject our love or render it ineffective. But when that happens, love has not failed. *People* have failed. Resorting to unloving behavior may get them temporary results, but in the long run, it's love that works.

Paul's letter to the church at Thessalonica is a good illustration of how love never fails. The only question is, Which expression of love best fits each situation we face? As Paul addresses the Thessalonians' problems, he makes reference to no less than sixteen different forms of love, highlighted by the phrase "one another."

One thing I appreciate so much about the Bible is that it is consistent. Concepts appearing in one place are reinforced in others. Love is no exception. In chapter 1 of this book we talked about love being the Great Com-

mandment. The condensed version of that commandment is "Love God and love people." Now, if you turn to
Paul's first letter to the church in Thessalonica, chapters
4 and 5, you'll find a treatise on loving people that is a
perfect complement to 1 Corinthians 13. It starts off with
a wonderfully positive exhortation.

> *Finally then, brethren, we request and exhort you in the Lord Jesus,*
> *that as you received from us instruction as to how you ought to*
> *walk and please God (just as you actually do walk), that you excel*
> *still more....*
>
> *Now, as to the love of the brethren, you have no need for anyone to*
> *write to you, for you yourselves are taught by God to love one another.*
> *(1 Thessalonians 4:1, 9)*

What follows in 1 Thessalonians is a series of "one
anothers," specific ways that you and I can practice
what Paul preaches. I've listed them below. Each one
gives us another way to express love, depending on the
need of the moment. Together they make a package that
will equip us to obey the exhortation, "Excel still more,"
a package which also helps assure that our "love never
fails." Take the time to look up each of the references.
Notice how many of the "one anothers" parallel the attributes of love found in 1 Corinthians 13. For example,
"rejoice with one another" could parallel "love rejoices
in the truth."

Comfort one another (4:18)
Encourage one another (5:11, 14)
Build up one another (5:11)
Appreciate one another (5:12)
Submit to one another (5:12)
Esteem (highly regard) one another (5:13)

Live in peace with one another (5:13)
Admonish one another (5:14)
Help one another (5:14)
Be patient with one another (5:14)
Don't repay evil for evil (5:15)
Seek good for one another (5:15)
Rejoice with one another (5:16)
Pray with one another (5:17)
Be thankful with one another (5:18)
Greet one another (5:26)

Love takes different forms for different occasions, and this list coupled with Paul's love letter illustrates the wealth of options at your disposal. The hard question to answer sometimes is which of these to use for which situation. Three additional and familiar "one anothers" provide a foundation from which to make these decisions.

BE DEVOTED TO ONE ANOTHER

The first question to ask is "Am I devoted to this person or to my own case or cause?" Romans 12:5 says, "So we, who are many, are one body in Christ, and individually members one of another." Then verse 10 goes on to say, "Be devoted to one another in brotherly love." The fact that we're connected to one another leads to the conclusion that I have to be devoted to you. I have an obligation to love you whether I like you or not, even if we hardly know one another. Why? Because we're part of one body, one family of God. This leads to a call for devotion, which means that love is loyal. It doesn't walk out.

BUILD ONE ANOTHER UP

The second key question is "What form of love will best build them up?" We've covered this admonition in the previous chapter, but it bears repeating here. Our source is Romans 14:19: "So then let us pursue the things which make for peace and the building up of one another." If you recall, the Greek word rendered here as "building up" means to move someone along toward spiritual maturity (remember the continuum diagram?). We should view every appointment in our lives as a divine appointment. When confronted with an opportunity to love, ask yourself, "What kind of response would help to move this person toward maturity in his or her walk with Christ?"

First Thessalonians 5:14 is a great one-verse proof that love takes different forms for different people at different points in their lives.

> We urge you, brethren, admonish the unruly, encourage the faint-hearted, help the weak, be patient with everyone.

Reaching out a helping hand isn't how you show love to an unruly person. He needs love that admonishes. Admonishment isn't the best way to lift the spirits of someone who's just had the wind taken out of his sails. He needs loving encouragement. In the same way that doctors prescribe certain medications to treat specific diseases, so the Scriptures prescribe certain responses to specific behaviors if we're to see relationships flourish. If you could bottle these responses and sell them at the pharmacy, they'd all be found on the aisle marked Love.

SERVE ONE ANOTHER

The final test to apply is "Do I have a servant spirit as I act?" Again, this is a familiar concept. Remember Philippians 2:3: "Do nothing from selfishness or empty conceit, but with humility of mind regard one another

as more important than yourselves"? Think again about
the waiter at that fine restaurant who we talked about
several chapters ago. If that guy walks in the door of the
restaurant each day saying to himself, "I'm here today to
serve people," he has laid a solid foundation for the deli-
cate task of giving each diner an excellent evening. Likewise, if we bring a servant's attitude to our dealings with
the people God brings our way, we're already positioned
to love them as He does—unconditionally.

As I go through life, I'm presented with all kinds of
opportunities to excel or fall flat at loving other people.
God wants me to excel and to do it freely. First John 4:11
says it powerfully:

> Beloved, if God so loved us, we also ought to love one another.

In response to God's love, freely given to us, we are
to give it freely to others. Again I find a great example of
this in Mother Teresa. She was once showing her work
to a wealthy celebrity who, overwhelmed I'm sure by it
all, said, "I couldn't do that for a million dollars," to
which Mother Teresa replied, "I couldn't either. But I
could do it for my Jesus. I could do it for the blood of
Christ. I could do it for the one who died for me." What
an important distinction. Don't love, don't do the "one
anothers" because they work. Do them for Jesus. Do
them in response to His love for you.

Where do you go to see what love that never fails
looks like? One place would be Judy and George Snider's
home. Over the past twenty years, love has had ample
opportunity to fail this remarkable couple. But it hasn't.
Judy has had multiple sclerosis for these past two decades. Hers is the aggressive form, and it quickly robbed
her of the ability to not only care for herself, but to do

almost anything. Judy is completely paralyzed. She can turn her head from side to side and speak softly. Nothing more.

When this insidious disease disabled George's wife and stole her strength, it could have taken his love away from her too. But theirs proved to be a love that never fails. Around-the-clock care was required, so George opted to quit work and go on disability to serve his wife rather than put her in a convalescent home. When a detached retina threatened to steal the sight from his right eye, George stubbornly refused hospitalization and surgery because Judy needed his daily help. (He finally relented when other caregivers stepped forward.) When he and Judy were given a weekend getaway in San Diego with various excursions arranged to accommodate them despite Judy's severe limitations, George was so exhausted from his eye surgery and caring for Judy that he just slept in their hotel room the entire weekend.

As for Judy's unfailing love, it prompted her to view the change of plans as a blessing. Instead of being disappointed at missing their planned activities, she simply said, "It gave George a whole weekend to sleep and relax. I think he needed that more after all he does to care for me." And you may be surprised to learn that Judy doesn't let their situation keep her from serving others. With a specially equipped telephone which she activates by blowing through a small tube, she makes all the weekly calls for the food fund, one of the helps ministries of our church.

Perhaps in their quiet moments Judy and George express their inner struggles to one another, or to their heavenly Father, but I've never heard a public word of complaint from either one of them. Each of them seems more concerned with the other one. For these two, "in sickness and in health" proved to be a vow that sealed their love not only at the altar, but for all time. And when I meet people like them, I have to agree with Paul's summary statement. Love never fails.

chapter thirteen

Love
Lasts Forever

LOVE'S ETERNAL VALUE

Invest in what will last. Don't get drawn into a fascination with cheap imitations that break records in the short run but break apart over the long haul. Invest in blue-chip stocks, those long-enduring companies that are here to stay.

This is sound financial advice, especially for the long-term investor who is expecting his money to grow and multiply for several decades. In the final section of his love letter, Paul gives us the same advice. Invest in what will last, he says. Keep your focus on the eternal, not the temporal. No matter how exciting gifts like prophecy, tongues, and knowledge may appear, they can't compare with love. Why not? Because love has staying power. Love will never go out of style. Love will be essential long after those other gifts have passed away. Love will be needed even after you reach full maturity. Love will be necessary even after faith and hope are replaced. Love, in a word, is eternal.

As Paul concluded his long list of the attributes of love, he made quite a statement. "Love never fails." What a claim! But it's true because love, unlike even faith and hope, will be fully functional—in gear and operating at top speed—through all eternity. In both style and substance it has staying power. Exercising love for God and others will never go out of style and will be a substantial part of our lives forever . . . and ever . . . and ever. So the final fact about the greatest thing in the universe is this:

Love is eternal. It never goes out of style.

In the conclusion of his letter (verses 8 through 12) Paul contrasts the permanence of love with the transitory, fleeting nature of all the spiritual gifts. He especially zeroes in on the more miraculous or public gifts, those which had attracted the attention of the church in Corinth. The Corinthians were no different from most Christians today. The church has always been enamored with the big show, the more showy gifts. The man or woman up front, on the mike, speaking or singing while others hang on every word. The one who can wax eloquent with smooth speech. The one who has amazing, perhaps supernatural insights into the events of the day. The one who can predict the future when the rest of us are trying to understand the past. God, on the other hand, has never been overly impressed with the supernatural. Maybe that's because He knows where the real power comes from. He's much more impressed with the simple acts of love just described in 1 Corinthians 13:4–7. He'll take a great lover over a great prophet or preacher any day of the week.

For I have been informed concerning you, my brethren, by Chloe's people, that there are quarrels among you. Now I mean this, that each one of you is saying, "I am of Paul," and "I of Apollos," and "I of Cephas," and "I of Christ." (1 Corinthians 1:11–12)

The Corinthian fascination with the public gifts, especially the supernatural gifts of the Spirit, is well documented throughout Paul's complete letter. At the very beginning (1:10–17) the apostle begins his epistle with a strong exhortation to grow up and quit following after men. The Corinthians had become divided among themselves, with each member of the church pledging allegiance to his favorite teacher. Some liked Apollos; others thought Cephas was the man. It wasn't just a matter of which radio station to tune into or which Christian book to browse and buy. This issue had believers fighting with one another. Quarrels were commonplace among this collection of immature believers. At the heart of their conflict was an unhealthy attraction, not just to men, but to their gifts. Gifts of knowledge, prophecy, perhaps even tongues were certainly part of the résumé for these great teachers. Paul himself admits in chapter 14 that he spoke in tongues as much as any of them, but he challenged their unhealthy fascination with the supernatural gifts of the Spirit.

Tongues—the supernatural ability to speak a language you have never learned—had become to the Corinthians the ultimate sign of spiritual maturity. They were so impressed with this gift and obsessed with possessing it that Paul devoted an entire section of his epistle (chapter 14) to an extended exhortation that they focus on gifts like prophecy instead of tongues. The church had gotten so out of balance that they thought everyone should seek this gift. Paul, therefore, points

out that none of the gifts are universally given to all believers (12:29–30). He then exhorts them to place their
emphasis on other gifts, like prophecy, that everyone
can understand (12:31a; 14:17– 19) and through which
they can be edified. But most of all, he offers them a
"more excellent way" (12:31b), a pursuit that is more
important than tongues, prophecy, or any divine gift.
The pursuit of love. Why? Because love, unlike these
temporary gifts, will last forever.

PROPHECY

If there are gifts of prophecy, they will be done away. (13:8a)

Prophecy—the supernatural ability to tell the future—will someday be "done away" with. The Greek
word used here, *katargeo,* means to be rendered idle or
useless. These gifts will "cease" (*New International Version*) or "fail" (King James Version). They will be abolished or destroyed, or have no effect or vanish. Get the
picture? Prophecy, by its very nature, is a temporary
gift. The prophet and his gift become useless once the
prophesied events have passed. The historian then takes
over for the prophet to help us look back on what was
once ahead of us. When history comes to completion,
then, the human story on planet earth is over as we
know it. Christ returns and establishes His new heaven
and new earth for all eternity. We live with Him and possess all knowledge, knowing "even as [we are] fully
known" (13:12 NIV). There will be no job openings for
prophets in such a world. Historians . . . maybe. Wor-
shipers . . . definitely. But prophets will need to find a
new line of work.

TONGUES

If there are tongues, they will cease. (13:8b)

Tongues are another gift that will pass with time. The Greek word here is *pauo*, which means "to stop" or "make an end." It is used primarily in the middle voice in the New Testament, which signifies a willing cessation. At some point in the future this gift of tongues will no longer be needed and will just "go away." The time of its cessation is uncertain. Perhaps the safest assumption is that it will pass away, along with prophecy and knowledge, when "the perfect comes" (13:10). The context of this paragraph would appear to support this position. Some would disagree, though, and point to the fact that *prophecy* and *knowledge* are specifically mentioned in verses 9 and 10 but *tongues* are not. They would also note that the verb tenses in verse 8 imply that prophecy and knowledge are forced to cease or be done away with, whereas tongues will cease on their own, willingly. This has led some commentators to conclude that the spiritual gift of tongues passes away before prophecy or knowledge. It is not the focus of this book to resolve all the issues surrounding the gift of tongues in the church today. But one fact is emphasized. Tongues will someday cease. One day tongues will no longer be an issue, for they will no longer be needed. But love will be in style and essential for all eternity.

THE PERFECT

When the perfect comes, the partial will be done away. (13:10)

The real point Paul appears to be making is that unlike love, all three of these gifts are temporary. They will be rendered useless "when the perfect comes." When is this coming of the "perfect"? To understand the verse, we must examine the term. The perfect, *teleios* in Greek, means complete. It comes from the word *telos,* or end, which is often used to describe spiritual maturity, such as in Matthew 5:48: "You are to be perfect as your heavenly Father is perfect." Ephesians speaks of the "mature man" (Ephesians 4:13) and of the "stature which belongs to the fullness of Christ." Hebrews tells of the "more perfect tabernacle," one not made with hands (Hebrews 9:11). James teaches that endurance in the midst of suffering completes or matures us in Christ, making us "perfect and complete, lacking in nothing" (James 1:4). The law of God is "perfect" in James 1:25, as are God's gifts in 1:17. Finally, in 1 John God's love is "perfect," or brought to completion, when it is not only received from above but also passed on to others (1 John 4:18).

The "perfect," then, pointed to by the apostle is that time when nothing is partial but all is complete (1 Corinthians 13:10). It is when we know, not in part, but just as we are known by God—fully and completely (13:12). It is when we no longer see "dimly" but then "face to face" (13:12). It is when we are with Jesus for all eternity. It is after Christ returns to complete all things, to establish His new heaven and new earth as the eternal dwelling place for believers of all time. And guess what? Prophecy, knowledge, and tongues will no longer be needed. The best prognosticators, wisest scholars, and most fluent linguists will be twiddling their thumbs and reading heaven's help-wanted ads.

Love, on the other hand, will be going and growing as never before. Like that Energizer bunny, it will keep going and going and going. Our love for the Savior will be fully active and energized by the presence of God. The more we know of Him, the more we will love Him. Love, you see, lasts forever.

Exactly when God brings the gifts of prophecy and knowledge to an end may be uncertain, but we know for sure that when Christ comes to complete history they'll no longer be needed. Likewise, the precise time when God allows the gift of tongues to pass away we cannot know, but we do know that once we are with our Lord, fully mature and perfected, there will be no need for the various human languages to be spoken. We will all speak the language of heaven, whatever tongue God ordains as the language of love in worship. First Corinthians 13, then, is not about the passing of any particular spiritual gifts, but about the permanence of love over all the temporary gifts of the Spirit.

Many have used this text to teach that once the Scriptures were completed, the miraculous gifts of the Spirit were to cease. We see from the context, however, that the "coming of the perfect" has nothing to do with the canon of Scripture. It points to our face-to-face encounter with Christ when He completes all things. That is not to say that all gifts must be fully functional at all times in all places. It is up to the sovereign purposes of God to distribute spiritual gifts to whomever He chooses, whenever He chooses, and wherever He chooses, for the advancement of His kingdom. First Corinthians 12:11 clearly states that the Spirit makes those choices "just as He wills." Chapter 13 leaves open the questions of when these gifts are abolished. He leaves no doubt that long after they are gone, love will remain.

The ongoing debate about spiritual gifts is indeed an important one. Every disciple of Jesus, every student or teacher of God's Word, should study the whole of Scripture, develop his or her convictions, and stand ready to defend them. But let us not forget that any position on spiritual gifts held or defended *without love* is "but a noisy gong or a clanging cymbal." Even if I "know all mysteries" and score 100 percent on heaven's theological exam, "but do not have love, I am nothing" (vv. 2–3).

LOVE IS GREATER THAN THE GREATEST VIRTUE

But now faith, hope, love, abide these three;
but the greatest of these is love. (13:13)

Paul concludes his love letter with one final declaration. "But now faith, hope, love, abide these three; but the greatest of these is love." He shifts his focus from spiritual gifts to spiritual virtues. Not only is love greater than the greatest gifts, it's also greater than the greatest virtues. Why? Because even faith and hope are temporary, but love is eternal!

But now faith abides (v. 13a). Faith is always esteemed in Scripture. We are exhorted to grow in faith, to exercise our faith, to stretch our faith. It is an essential muscle of the spiritually fit soul. True spirituality is impossible without it. The New Testament letter of Hebrews says it is impossible to please God unless we have it. Faith is the basis of entry into the "Hall of Faith" in Hebrews 11. Making it into this chapter is like being inducted into the shrines of Akron or Cooperstown or getting your star on Hollywood's walk of fame. So maybe faith is love's equal or even love's superior. After all, according to Ephesians 2:8–9, we are saved by grace through faith plus nothing. But Paul still places faith below love. Why? Again, the issue is permanence. Hebrews declares that faith is "the assurance of things hoped for, the conviction of things not seen"(Hebrews 11:1). Once the perfect comes, though, once we experience our full redemption in Christ, once we see Him face-to-face, faith will no longer be essential. The future will be now. Our dreams, nurtured and held secure by faith, will be reality. Faith will fade away, but love will still rule our hearts. In fact, as the focus of our faith is fully realized, our love will be energized and elevated to new heights. The reason is simple. Because Jesus Christ, up close and personal, will exceed all of our dreams and expectations.

But now hope abides (v. 13*b*). Hope, likewise, is a great virtue. When God inspired the apostle to write to the churches, the apostle always highlighted the strength or weakness of their hope. The hope of which Paul speaks, however, one of the three great virtues, is nothing like our contemporary concept of "hope." Today's use of this term usually conveys a note of skepticism and doubt. To say, "Well, I hope so," suggests you're looking for a long shot at best.

New Testament hope, though, *elpis* in the Greek, wasn't about doubt or skepticism. Rather, it was an expression of assurance and confidence. Our hope is "fixed in heaven." We have a sure and certain hope, a future home, full of riches in Christ that we can count on, anticipate, and even celebrate before they are realized. This is because our hope is constructed of the eternal reliable promises of God. Its future delivery is guaranteed, prepaid in full with a generous tip by the blood of Christ on the cross. When it comes to my hope being there for me, the Father, the Son, and the Holy Spirit all promise, "We deliver!" And once delivered, this hope will not disappoint like some things we hope for in this life.

I'll never forget the first time I ever went to the circus. I anticipated for weeks the fun I'd have. And I saved my money so I could buy all the souvenirs I wanted, absolutely convinced that they'd become instant treasures, my most prized possessions. Well, the circus was fun, but most of my delight disappeared when I got home, laid my new circus toys on my bed, and realized that they were no more than a bunch of trinkets that had cost me far more than they were worth. Sometimes the dream *is* better than the reality.

But our God and heaven's joys will never disappoint. The finite mind cannot conceive of the beauty and joy of eternity with God in heaven. So nurture the dream. Keep your hope in focus, and it will keep you on track day by day. Living with a clear and certain hope in front of you will keep you going even in the toughest of times, like Jesus, who "for the joy set before Him endured the cross" (Hebrews 12:2). That joy was His certain hope of again being seated with His Father, having accomplished His mission of redemption.

As with faith, though, once our hopes have been realized, they become part of our history. In one sense, you could say that hope self-destructs after it is realized. It becomes history to be celebrated instead of events to be anticipated. God wants us to know and live in light of our hope and calling in Christ and to know the riches of our inheritance with the saints (Ephesians 1:18). But once that inheritance is ours, hope is no longer relevant. Once salvation and glorification are secured and experienced fully, hope, like faith, is obsolete. You see, even the "death" of my hope breathes more life into my love. As all I've dreamed of in Christ moves from hope to reality, my love keeps right on going. It not only survives but thrives and even multiplies as my hopes are fulfilled and experienced. To paraphrase verse 12, "Now we hope in a mirror dimly, but then face to face." My love grows deeper and stronger as I now "know fully just as I also have been fully known." Love, meanwhile, remains for eternity. No wonder Paul declares, "The greatest of these is love."

What should we remember from this profound section? I'd offer a few concluding suggestions.

Love, not spiritual gifts, should be our pursuit and our passion. First Corinthians 14:1 flows from the truths of 1 Corinthians 13 and declares, "Pursue love, yet desire earnestly spiritual gifts." Even though you may desire spiritual gifts, don't pursue them. Pursue only love. Spiritual gifts will take care of themselves. God will give you what you need, or better yet, just what the body of Christ needs from you. Paul begins chapter 13 by declaring that without love, even the most extreme degrees of giftedness are useless to God. And he ends the chapter by placing love over every gift and every spiritual virtue in life.

Love, along with faith and hope, is a great measure of maturity. The focus of 1 Corinthians 13 is clearly on love as the Great Commandment and the great essential for a Christian life that is pleasing to God. But as we've just discussed, we dare not minimize the importance of love's two companions in verse 13, faith and hope. In one short verse God reminds us that faith and hope share a unique place, along with love, in the heart of God. Love may be king of the virtues, but faith and hope certainly reign at its side. In fact, when I exercise my faith—build it strong—my love is strengthened as well. When I meditate on the hope I have in Christ, my love grows deeper. Conversely, if my faith is weak and my hope out of focus, my love will wane as well. My affections will be drawn away from Christ and other people by this world which I can see and touch. Remember, "now faith, hope, love, abide *these three*" (emphasis added).

Love will never go out of style, even in eternity. Knowledge, tongues, prophecy, even faith and hope, will become null and void, but love will not. Love can grow through all eternity as we experience the presence of God. As we worship our Savior, as we come into the presence of the Father, the Son, and the Holy Spirit, we must always remember that we will be nothing without love. Love will motivate our worship, energize our praise, and overflow into acts of service and obedience in joy. Love will grow for eternity because our God is eternally worthy of our affections.

In the 1960s the rock opera *Godspell* gave us a song that has stuck with me over the years. The lyrics of the tune "Day by Day" are like a prayer. They ask for three things: that we might "see Thee more clearly . . . love Thee more dearly . . . and follow Thee more nearly day by day." There is a nugget of truth found in the order of this trio of requests. As we see God more clearly, we will grow to love Him more dearly. Why? Because God is fully worthy of our love and affection. He is a lovely God. As we get to know Him "up close and personal," face-to-face, we will grow in our love and adoration for Him. Because He is eternally lovable, I doubt that I will ever exhaust my capacity for loving Him. Then, as I love Him more dearly, following Him more nearly will come easily. Obedience is always a joy when it comes out of an experience of grace.

No wonder Paul wrote that the greatest of these is love. He knew that love lasts forever.

chapter fourteen

Getting Started: A Perspective on Growing in Love

ASSEMBLY REQUIRED

When Becky and I were parents of preschoolers, that special day came when we bought our first swing set for the kids. You may be familiar with the routine. You get home from the store and remove the *unassembled* swing set—in its box—from the trunk of the car with a mixture of fear, trembling, and eager anticipation. As I tore into the contents with my usual reckless abandon, I stumbled across the directions and uncharacteristically decided to read them. I'll never forget what they had to say.

First came a list of the tools I'd need to do this job: pliers, screwdriver, and wrenches. Next came an admonition to read the *entire* list of instructions before commencing with the assembly. Third was the estimated time to complete the job, and this is where the technical writer assigned to produce these particular instructions absolutely made my day. Here's what he or she had written:

Assembly time if done alone: 3 hours
Assembly time if done with two small helpers: 8 hours

Isn't that hilarious? Fact is, I'm notorious for launching into a project unprepared. My motto is "Jump in with both feet and it'll all work out OK." Trouble is, halfway through the project I usually realize that I don't have all the tools required for the job or I've messed up the assembly sequence. Don't worry, I'm learning.

As our study of 1 Corinthians 13 and its divine description of love comes to a close, I'm left with one final fear. It's that you, having put your mind to the study of love, having dissected its components, analyzed its parts, and learned of its incredible importance, might close this book and rush out eager to love as described in this remarkable chapter. Ready to try harder, you're convinced that this time you'll make it happen. You're going to make yourself into the most loving man, woman, or kid on the planet!

Before you start assembly, though, or reassemble your "love life," God's Word would remind you to slow down. First Corinthians 13 gives us the nuts and bolts of a love that never fails. It always works. You could even say it "swings." But before tackling this project, make sure you have the tools it takes to complete it successfully.

From some other chapters in God's instruction manual, the Bible, I would highlight four truths worth remembering before you begin this vital assembly process.

TRUTH #1
LOVE IS OF GOD, NOT MAN, SO GET CONNECTED

If you hope to grow in your ability to love, we've seen that you have to get connected to God. A commitment to loving Him will have a ripple effect on all of life's rela-

tionships—with friends, family, and neighbors. Our blue-
print is found in 1 John 4:7–13.

From the passage we can make three significant observations.

> *Beloved, let us love one another, for love is from God; and everyone who loves is born of God and knows God. The one who does not love does not know God, for God is love. By this the love of God was manifested in us, that God has sent His only begotten Son into the world so that we might live through Him. In this is love, not that we loved God, but that He loved us and sent His Son to be the propitiation for our sins. (1 John 4:7–10)*

Love is rooted in God's character. We're far too inclined to base our assessment of a person's love on what
the person does. This is especially inappropriate when it
comes to God's love. It says in verse 8 that "God is love."
It's not just because of His conduct that He is love; it's
because of His character. Love is rooted in who He is.
His conduct then flows out of His character. Because
God is love . . . God loves.

> *Beloved, if God so loved us, we also ought to love one another. No one has seen God at any time; if we love one another, God abides in us, and His love is perfected in us. (1 John 4:11–12)*

Love is a reflection of God's presence. Verses 9 through
13 make it clear that our love flows out of God's presence
in us. "Everyone who loves is born of God and knows
God," we see in verse 7. If we really love the way God
loves, John says, we reflect His presence to other people.
I don't know about you, but I find this to be immensely
encouraging, because it tells me that God's love is trans-
ferable. It can be developed and lived out in my life.

> *By this we know that we abide in Him and He in us, because He has given us of His Spirit. (1 John 4:13)*

Love is a result of God's power. As the Holy Spirit of God lives in and through me, as I abide in Christ and walk with Him, I can expect God's type of love to be evident in my life. As He leads the way, then His power can flow through me.

If you've ever watched or been involved in automotive racing or competitive cycling, you're familiar with the term *drafting*. It's a technique for gaining an advantage over a competitor by slipping into the wind stream he creates as he slices through the air. Drafting can save much needed fuel or energy, which may prove invaluable later in the race. The beauty of the technique is that you win by using the energy of the person in front of you.

Loving God's way is like drafting. Our capacity to love flows from Him, not from self-effort, and as we tap into His power we are equipped and energized to love like Paul calls us to love. So if we're serious about building love into our lives, we need to lay a foundation that is grounded in God.

There are several implications to the three observations we've just listed. The first is that *apart from Christ I can never become the lover God wants me to be.* Loving is not about trying harder; it's about abiding in Christ. When I abide in Him, I rely on His power, not my own.

Implication number two is that *loving is linked as much to who I am as to what I do.* The reason God is such a great Lover is that He is love. He wants to abide in us so that He can change who we are, a change that will be reflected in what we do. A view from the opposite perspective underscores this point. If love is reduced to simply what I do and not who I am, if I'm always trying to do something that I am not, eventually I'll burn out. However, if what I'm doing is a reflection of what I'm becoming, it's more natural and, at times, even easier. It's much more natural to be a loving servant-husband if God is remaking me on the inside into more of a loving servant-person. Then I can live out love in my marriage. I think far too much attention is being given these days to principles for having a good home, or principles for communication, or principles for communicating the language of love apart from the realization that if I'm not growing in my relationship with God, then all those principles are doomed to long-term failure. God wants me to become a certain kind of person first so that I am then able to do the hard work of loving.

A final implication is that *I need to focus on my spiritual life,* which is the key to success in the rest of my life. When I'm growing spiritually, I become a more loving person even if I never study love the rest of my life. Why? Because the first fruit of the Spirit of God is love.

TRUTH #2
LOVE IS AN ACT, NOT A FEELING, SO JUST DO IT

There comes a point when we need to realize that love cannot be linked to feelings because that's not God's approach.

> *Little children, let us not love with word or with tongue, but in deed and truth. (1 John 3:18)*

I'd paraphrase this as "loving with action and sincerity," which suggests that love is a behavior we choose (dare I say even when we don't feel like it?). We live in a society that screams at us the misconception that love is something I feel, something I fall into, or something that captures me. One author says that "love is the feeling you get when you get a feeling you never felt before."

Remember when I thought I was "in love" and contemplating marrying Becky, I talked with a pastor because I wasn't sure how to read my feelings. "How do I know that this thing is real?" I asked him. His reply: "You'll just know it." But I didn't know it. Love may be a feeling you get when you get a feeling you never felt before, but I have a lot of feelings I've never felt before, and a lot of them aren't remotely close to love. Indigestion, maybe, but not love.

Love generates feelings, but it is not at its core a feeling. At its core love is built on character, which we see reflected in our actions. It is reflected in how I choose to behave. Nowhere is this illustrated more clearly than through Jesus' own words.

> *"You have heard that it was said, 'You shall love your neighbor and hate your enemy.' But I say to you, love your enemies and pray for those who persecute you, so that you may be sons of your Father who is in heaven; for He causes His sun to rise on the evil and the good, and sends rain on the righteous and the unrighteous. For if you love those who love you, what reward do you have? Do not even the tax collectors do the same? If you greet only your brothers, what more are you doing than others? Do not even the Gentiles do the same? Therefore you are to be perfect, even as your heavenly Father is perfect." (Matthew 5:43–48)*

When Jesus says I'm to love my enemies, He translates love as an action, not a feeling. Nowhere in Scripture do I see God saying that when you run into your enemies, you ought to feel excited about seeing them. When was the last time you saw someone greet their enemies with a big hug and a hearty "Oh, I missed you so much!"? To do so seems ridiculous. That's not a common response to someone who talks you down or lies to you. Jesus knows you don't feel like loving people who treat you that way. So when He says, "Love your enemies," He's not talking about feelings. He's talking about intentional behavior.

If love is being kind to someone who doesn't deserve it, if love is forgiving someone who doesn't deserve it, if love is passing up an opportunity to embarrass someone in front of other people when she *does* deserve it, if love is treating someone far better than he or she deserves to be treated, then *love is an action.* It's choosing to do something even if emotionally I don't feel like doing it. If you're going to love your enemies, you have to do so in spite of your feelings.

Some might charge that this type of "love" is hypocritical. The Bible says to "let love be without hypocrisy" (Romans 12:9), and isn't it hypocritical to act nice to someone you don't like? No, it's not. A hypocrite is someone who pretends to be something he's *not,* which is much different from someone who does something he *ought.* When I choose to do something I ought to do regardless of my feelings, that honors God. It's not hypocritical.

This discussion demands that we address another question. Does love have *anything* to do with feelings? You bet it does. The Scriptures make it clear that love *produces* feelings. Proverbs tells a husband to "rejoice in the wife of your youth" (5:18). Note that it doesn't say, "Do right by the wife of your youth." It says I'm supposed to get excited! In fact, it gets even better. The next verse says to "be exhilarated always with her love." The Hebrew word for "exhilarate" means to be drunk with her love. I'm to be a little bit crazy in my love for my wife. That's what I call an exhortation to let your feelings run deep.

I'll have to admit that I have trouble tolerating the unbiblical view that love is *only* about commitment. Of course it's about commitment—expressed in action. It is expressed by what I do, but not to the exclusion of all feelings.

Pulling these two ends of this actions/feelings spectrum together, here's a summary. There is a healthy dimension to the feeling side of love. God gave us feelings, but they are not the foundation of our love relationships. Feelings make great followers but lousy leaders. When it comes to love, regardless of your feelings, do what you know to be right, and in the process your feelings will often be revived and renewed.

Cain and Abel's story illustrates this point. If you recall, Cain murdered Abel. God knew it, yet when He came to Cain, this is what He said:

> *"Why are you angry? And why has your countenance fallen? If you do well, will not your countenance be lifted up? And if you do not do well, sin is crouching at the door; and its desire is for you, but you must master it." (Genesis 4:6–7)*

Countenance means "facial expression." God comes to Cain, knowing what he has done, and asks why he's so sad. Then, in the same breath, tells him that if he does what is right, he'll get his joy back. The feeling, *joy,* will follow the action, *doing what is right.*

TRUTH #3
LOVE IS A GIFT, NOT A WAGE OR A BRIBE,
SO GIVE IT FREELY

As I studied a passage in the gospel of Luke recently, I saw it in an entirely different light. Here it is.

"If you love those who love you, what credit is that to you? For even sinners love those who love them. If you do good to those who do good to you, what credit is that to you? For even sinners do the same. If you lend to those from whom you expect to receive, what credit is that to you? Even sinners lend to sinners in order to receive back the same amount. But love your enemies, and do good, and lend, expecting nothing in return; and your reward will be great, and you will be sons of the Most High; for He Himself is kind to ungrateful and evil men. Be merciful, just as your Father is merciful. Do not judge, and you will not be judged; and do not condemn, and you will not be condemned; pardon, and you will be pardoned. Give, and it will be given to you. They will pour into your lap a good measure—pressed down, shaken together, and running over. For by your standard of measure it will be measured to you in return." (Luke 6:32–38)

While this verse is often used, and accurately so, to teach about financial giving, notice that its context is a discussion about the nature of love. It is not just a treatise on money. Jesus is saying that if we give love, we'll get love in return. In fact, you'll get back even more than you give. That's a biblical principle. Notice also in verse 32 how Jesus' words fly in the face of our culture today: "If you love those who love you, what credit is that to you? For even sinners love those who love them." That is what I call love given as a wage. Conditional love. Love that says I'm loving you because you did something for me. My love is a payback. (Isn't that how love is so often given today?) Jesus says that's wrong. Love is to be a *gift*, not a *wage*.

Another abuse of love is to give it as a *bribe*. We see that in verse 34, which talks about love that expects something in return.

"If you lend to those from whom you expect to receive, what credit is that to you? Even sinners lend to sinners in order to receive back the same amount."

This is describing love given by a wife expecting her husband or kids to shape up. It's love given by a husband expecting his wife to reciprocate. It's love given to a coworker or friend anticipating a dividend of some sort later on. Jesus says to give expecting nothing in return. The irony is that if your love is a gift, freely given, you'll eventually get a return on your investment. But if payback is your motive, you lose double. Both the joy of loving and the desired return will elude you.

TRUTH #4
LOVE IS AN OBLIGATION, NOT AN OPTION, SO PAY IT

Romans 13:8 tells us to "owe nothing to anyone." This is another section of Scripture that's commonly used to teach a principle of financial management, with good reason. But notice again that the context provided by the rest of the verse reveals that its primary focus is something different.

> *Owe nothing to anyone except to love one another; for he who loves his neighbor has fulfilled the law.*

Love is a *debt,* according to this text. It's the only legitimate debt we should carry. We should live with the attitude that love is not optional. It's obligatory. This is one debt we need to pay, freely, every time it comes due. The same idea is found later on in the New Testament:

> *Beloved, if God so loved us, we also ought to love one another. (1 John 4:11)*

That word *ought* is not a take-it-or-leave-it suggestion. It indicates an obligation to love one another in response to God's love for us. Understanding Christianity and understanding the uniqueness of God's grace should spur us to love. The message of Christianity is that God doesn't love us because we first loved Him. By grace He chose to love us first. And if the love of God has been showered upon me by grace, then logic suggests that I have an obligation to love other people by that same grace model. I would go so far as to say that it is immoral to hoard the love of God, which we did absolutely nothing to deserve.

Loving Must Be Grown, So Nurture It

When was the last time you wrote a letter anticipating that one day people would study it word by word, picking apart all of its key ideas and analyzing its most intimate phrases? My guess is never. And I think Paul would be surprised at all the attention people like you and me have paid to his letter to the Corinthian church over the centuries. Granted, the words were written under the inspiration of the Holy Spirit. But if Paul had known of our future interest, I wonder if he might not have lobbied to conclude with a brief footnote, something like *Love is like a garden. If you want it to grow, you should tend to it regularly.*

Now wait a minute, you protest. Didn't you say just a few pages back that love is of God? And doesn't that mean that once we get a grip on God's love, we're always able to do it well? Yes, love is of God, but He never says it's something we master. Oh, we may get good at it. Perhaps very good. Like the church at Thessalonica. When writing to them, Paul told them he was "constantly bearing in mind your work of faith and labor of love," and that they "be-came an example to all the believers in Macedonia and in Achaia" (1 Thessalonians 1:3, 7). When it came to loving, these folks had it down. But after praising their passion, listen to how Paul challenges them.

> Now may our God and Father Himself and Jesus our Lord direct our way to you; and may the Lord cause you to increase and abound in love for one another, and for all people, just as we also do for you. (1 Thessalonians 3:11–12)

Isn't that fascinating? Not only does Paul tell this group of exceptional Christians to "increase and abound in love," he also makes clear that a growing, maturing love is what he wants in his own life and the lives of those closest to him. It's evident here that we who are intent on loving are in for a lifelong project. From the tenor of Paul's words, love is something we should never stop working on.

As if this weren't a high enough expectation, not many verses later we discover that the goal is not only to love *more*, to *keep on growing* in our capacity to love, but also to love better.

> Now as to the love of the brethren, you have no need for anyone to write to you, for you yourselves are taught by God to love one another; for indeed you do practice it toward all the brethren who are in all Macedonia. But we urge you, brethren, to excel still more. (1 Thessalonians 4:9–10)

Read these verses again and let their message settle into your soul. Paul is writing to the one church in Asia that had a triple-A love rating. They were doing it well and "practicing" to get even better. And Paul was obviously pleased with their progress. His long-term goal for them, however, was not a fixed point somewhere down the line, some point at which they'd be masters of godly loving. No, what Paul envisioned for the Thessalonians, and what he would hope for us as well, is that we "excel still more." Keep on growing in your love. Never stop. That's the desire of Paul's heart.

How do we make it the desire of our hearts? How do we abound still more? I have an idea. Instead of just tossing his love letter in a drawer with the other New Testament letters now that we're through reading it, what if we leave it out where we can see it every day. Maybe put a special marker on it. Then each time you glance at that marker, bring to mind something you learned as we read through Paul's words together. If some days your memories get a little fuzzy, flip your Bible open to that special letter and slowly read it again. Be reminded of Paul's mission in life—to love the Lord his God and to love his neighbor as himself.

Above all, whenever you find yourself reflecting on one of the love lessons you learned from Paul, don't just make it a mental exercise. Conclude your review session by making those words of Jesus your next assignment.

"Go and do likewise."

REVIEW AND STUDY GUIDE

James S. Bell Jr.

Chapter One

1. The entire moral instruction of the Old and New Testaments centers around love—for both God and our neighbor.

2. Whatever we try to achieve in communication, if the words are not accompanied by love, they will not reach their mark.

3. Though knowledge is important, a strong relationship based upon love is more important because it reflects the character of the Trinity.

4. Love is centered on others and therefore requires a service that is sacrificial—requiring time, effort, and the best we have to offer of ourselves.

QUESTIONS AND RESPONSE

1. Find a few examples in the Bible of moral instruction that may not mention love directly but have a clear association nonetheless. What does this mean for you? What do you need to do?

2. When have you been guilty of substituting spiritual knowledge as a means to spiritual growth over and above the obligation to love others? How did others respond? How does this affect your spiritual life?

3. Especially in times of stress and tragedy, love is a needed bond drawing people together and drawing them to the source of its power. How has this come into play in your life?

Chapter Two

1. Patience is the ability to wait without seeking change that benefits you, and expecting that the best outcome will occur eventually.

2. Nagging and pushing others is an unwillingness to trust God that His timing in their lives will accomplish the objective He seeks.

3. If impatience is an attempt to push people toward a desired end, then kindness is the willingness to help them toward that same end.

4. To practice effective kindness we need to take the initiative; that is, we need to notice and respond to the many needs of others, even if they inconvenience us.

5. Similar to the Good Samaritan, we need to surprise others with kindness when they least expect or deserve it.

QUESTIONS AND RESPONSE

1. When have you been most blessed with a random act of kindness? When did you most enjoy doing this for someone else?

2. In what areas do you find it most difficult to express patience? Do anxiety, anger, manipulation, or other sins manifest themselves instead?

3. How can you respond to someone's physical needs? Emotional? Spiritual? Can you think of a time when someone responded to yours in a Christlike manner?

Chapter Three

1. Jealousy is a wild and cruel emotion that seeks to harm the object of its affection because of mistrust and possessiveness.

2. To counteract jealousy, choose trust instead, and you will not drive away the one you cherish and who cherishes you.

3. Our natural tendency in a culture of broken promises is to try to control and supervise others, but that will not heal broken relationships or make others comply.

4. Envy is closely related to jealousy and seeks to possess what we don't have as opposed to being content ourselves and blessing the success of others.

5. Love builds up others, but envy seeks to take and also to destroy what others have, rather than be content.

QUESTIONS AND RESPONSE

1. In what areas do you struggle the most with jealousy or envy, and how does that point to your lack of contentment in those areas?

2. What barriers have built up in your relationships because of jealousy or envy, and how can you rectify this?

3. How can you learn to trust someone who has/hasn't disappointed you in the past?

Chapter Four

1. Bragging reflects an attitude of arrogance that makes you the final word on every topic and puts the focus on your accomplishments.

2. To be a lover rather than a braggart means entering into the minds and hearts of others, being truly interested in their achievements rather than your own.

3. Critical words spoken about someone in front of others will seriously hurt a relationship, whereas compliments strongly build up that same relationship.

4. Arrogance blows us up beyond our true worth, but love inflates and builds up the other person, helping to achieve what God intends for our neighbor.

5. The opposite of arrogance is humility, a willingness to admit and attack our shortcomings, rather than exaggerate our accomplishments.

QUESTIONS AND RESPONSE

1. When have you known you were wrong, and yet still couldn't admit it? How does love overcome this weakness and what is the outcome?

2. Name some of your inherent character weaknesses in different situations that might tempt you to brag about your achievements. Do you need to admit to someone that you are/were wrong?

3. How can you show someone you love that you are putting him or her before yourself?

Chapter Five

1. Good manners have gone out of style and appear to be outdated, old-fashioned gestures to some—mere window dressing or artificial aspects of a relationship.

2. Polite words and gestures are instinctive in courtship but tend to be discarded somewhat in the familiarity of marriage.

3. Each verbal expression connected with good manners denotes an awareness of another's feelings and appreciation for them rather than manipulation for our own ends.

4. "Please" and "thank you" are easy compared to "you go first," which signals in a variety of ways that our servant heart truly yields to others' needs.

5. The toddler's property laws——in every situation, claim everything for self—are the model for immaturity in manners.

QUESTIONS AND RESPONSE

1. Some claim that constant politeness is not sincerity and is overformal. How would you respond?

2. What gestures, mannerisms, words, and actions do you most respect and admire in a specific person? Why?

3. If you are married, what are some things you need to bring back into your relationship?

Chapter Six

1. Unselfishness means putting others' needs first regardless of your own, whether they are insignificant or life threatening.

2. To seek the interests of others implies a radical obedience that demands everything—potentially the death of all your own desires.

3. Being a servant does not mean you are a weak person; instead, God uses your strengths and talents to meet the needs of others.

4. True service does not seek any recognition from people whatsoever because its motivation is to please and glorify God and experience His pleasure.

5. Sometimes the best way to glorify God is through bad situations—serving others who don't appreciate us and don't immediately reciprocate.

Questions and Response

1. When were you asked to serve in a situation where there was no reward to you and yet God provided an unexpected reward? How did you respond?

2. Name the strengths you have that can be used to serve others. What is holding you back? What can you do to get rid of those things?

3. Who do you know who has served without recognition? How can you encourage him or her?

Chapter Seven

POINTS TO CONSIDER

1. To allow yourself to be provoked means to be tempted to speak damaging words and engage in actions that could have devastating consequences.

2. We are most motivated to deal with anger when we see the damage it can cause if we allow it to control us, rather than vice versa.

3. If you allow anger to either build or fester due to a number of unresolved issues, you will not be able to deal rationally with the causes first.

4. You need to review carefully how you normally deal with intense feelings of anger —and why—to be better able to keep anger from escalating into sin.

5. Anger is a response that involves wrong motivations, inappropriate timing, and a destructive attitude—all of which can be adjusted positively.

QUESTIONS AND RESPONSE

1. How do you normally respond when provoked? Do you seek to "get even," or do you react in love?

2. Within the last year, what situations brought out both your best responses in anger as well as your worst?

3. What anger needs to be resolved in your life? Is this important enough for you to try to resolve your anger today?

Chapter Eight

1. Mercy is withholding judgment and punishment, whereas grace is giving something positive when it is not deserved.

2. Because God continually forgives us, we should do likewise, though it is only a small portion of the favor shown to us.

3. A lack of forgiveness can cause us to distance ourselves from God as well as to allow bitterness to enter our lives, instead of the opportunity to love and worship Him.

4. Even if the other party does not seek reconciliation, forgiveness is a choice we alone make to wipe the debt out of our lives and no longer remember it.

5. There are many strong excuses not to forgive—we still hurt, it's impossible to forget, or there are huge consequences—but none of these will suffice.

Questions and Response

1. Is there bitterness in your life from the inability or unwillingness to forgive? Name one incident in your life when you found forgiveness to be impossible. Have you forgiven the offender yet? If not, what excuse do you give?

2. Explain the difference between mercy and grace, especially in a way that relates to others' actions toward you.

Chapter Nine

1. We need to be honest when wronged; and though we don't retaliate, we don't condone that same unrighteous behavior.

2. Never compromise with unrighteousness, but always be willing to expose unrighteousness with the sharp sword of the truth before it overcomes you.

3. When offended, we can be honest about the hurt, straightforward about the consequences, confrontational about truth, and yet hopeful for positive change.

4. Today it is often difficult to deal with the truth of an issue when encountering unrighteous behavior because our culture no longer holds absolute notions of moral right and wrong.

5. Today, because of the breakdown in the belief that there is absolute truth, we confuse love with tolerance and are told we are judgmental if we condemn sins such as homosexuality.

QUESTIONS AND RESPONSE

1. How in the past have you walked the fine line between loving the sinner and somehow excusing or not speaking out against the sin? What were the results of your inaction?

2. Give some examples of tolerance of others' behavior or beliefs that appear to be compassionate but actually promote compromise or lack of courage. How do you defend an approach of "intolerance"?

Chapter Ten

1. Irritations, imperfections, and irregularities are those out-of-the-ordinary things in life due to a fallen world that must be borne and tolerated if we are to love well.

2. We can sometimes tolerate the behavior of others without responding positively, but that is not true evidence of a genuinely forbearing spirit.

3. The simple communication to someone that you truly believe in him or her can become their greatest motivation to succeed.

4. When we build up others for the common good, we ultimately help ourselves as well as all those who come into contact with that other person.

5. All of us are at different points along the spiritual growth spectrum, and as we recognize this we can help each person to advance toward a mature faith, one step at a time.

Questions and Response

1. Encouraging and supporting others doesn't take a lot of effort. What most holds you back?

2. Identify the irritations or flaws in others that cause you to react negatively. How can you change? How can you respond in a way that builds them up?

3. When has someone supported you in a tough circumstance? How did it affect you?

Chapter Eleven

1. In today's world it is easy to lose hope when our expectations are not met, our dreams die, or relationships fall apart.

2. Because God is reliable, faithful, and unchanging, we can always depend upon His help, knowing that the outcome is completely in His hands and will work for our good.

3. Reviewing God's promises is perhaps the best way to restore hope, so we should meditate upon them and believe that the God who stands behind them will never let us down.

4. Endurance in relationships may not have all the excitement or personal recognition that personal success often includes, but it is far more satisfying if you stay the course.

5. If we first bear difficulties and continue to hope in the face of failure, we will be much more able to endure and persist in a loving way.

Questions and Response

1. Are you the type of person who wants to quit in the face of disappointment and pain, or do you by habit take these as a matter of course in order to finish your commitment?

2. Look up the most appropriate promises of God for the greatest difficulties you face. What do they say to you? How should you respond to God's promises?

Chapter Twelve

POINTS TO CONSIDER

1. If we cannot receive God's love through Jesus Christ, we will not be able to love others in the multiple and difficult ways outlined in 1 Corinthians 13.

2. "Love God and love your fellow human beings" are the commands that most please God and are taught by His Spirit, if He lives within us.

3. Devotion to one another means that we are obligated to meet each other's needs and are loyal to each other, even in difficult times when we are tempted to quit.

4. We often neglect to build each other up, which simply means taking the opportunity to express love and support. By so doing, we encourage each person to grow into maturity.

5. Serving each other should be done freely, with enthusiasm, and with the desire to excel in the task we undertake.

QUESTIONS AND RESPONSE

1. Where do you tend to draw the line when it comes to serving someone else unconditionally? What would motivate you in a greater way? Who do you need to love unconditionally? How will you show them?

2. We cannot meet the demands of devotion, encouragement, and service in our own strength. Seek God for His grace and power.

Chapter Thirteen

1. Most of the gifts God has given us, even spiritual gifts, are incomplete and will not last to eternity. The one exception is love.

2. Though faith and hope are of permanent value, unlike love, we will no longer need them when we see Him face-to-face.

3. Prophecy and tongues only point to perfect knowledge and therefore must end when all temporal events come to pass and we know Him in full.

4. Our focus should not be on pursuing spiritual gifts, even though they may be beneficial. Instead we should pursue love, which has eternal significance.

5. We should pray to see God more clearly; thus we will be able to serve and follow Him better each day.

QUESTIONS AND RESPONSE

1. If spiritual gifts truly help other people in terms of their eternal destinies, why don't these gifts have the same lasting value as love?

2. Explain how even though faith is essential, and faith and hope are eternal in their nature, yet love is the telling feature of the follower of Christ.

Chapter Fourteen

1. Love, because it comes from the character of God and results from His power, can only be obtained by abiding in Him and letting His life flow through us.

2. Often we think that love is a set of good feelings about someone else, but love is best expressed by the actions that respond to those feelings.

3. Loving your enemies is not about feelings but chosen behavior—treating them better than they deserve and not retaliating in response to their offenses.

4. Love is not paying someone back or earning something. It is giving even when the other does not deserve it, because we are obliged to do it for the sake of Christ.

5. We need to use the grace model in loving others, giving away God's love because we didn't deserve it in the first place.

QUESTIONS AND RESPONSE

1. Think back to times when others gave you love that you never deserved. How can you pass that same spirit on to others who don't deserve your love?

2. When have you confused freely loving others with receiving at least something positive in return? How does this conflict with the grace model?

3. To whom do I need to give God's love? How can I do that? What are the consequences if I don't?